DEFIANT
AND
DISMASTED
AT TRAFALGAR

Other books by Mary McGrigor

History of South Lochaweside

Dalmally and the Glens

Argyll Land of Blood and Beauty

'Grass will not grow on my grave' –the story of the
'Appin Murder' in 1752

History of the Family of Edmonstone of Duntreath *(edited)*

The Scalpel and the Sword. Autobiography of Sir James McGrigor,
father of the R.A.M.C *(edited)*

Rob Roy's Country

DEFIANT AND DISMASTED AT TRAFALGAR

by

MARY McGRIGOR

based on the original biography of
Sir William Hargood
by
James Allen
1841

LEO COOPER

First published in Great Britain 2004 by
LEO COOPER
an imprint of Pen & Sword Books,
47 Church Street, Barnsley
South Yorkshire, S70 2AS

Copyright © Mary McGrigor 2004

ISBN 1 84415 034 8

A CIP catalogue record for this book is
available from the British Library.

Typeset in 11/13pt Sabon by
Phoenix Typesetting, Auldgirth, Dumfriesshire.

Printed and bound by
CPI UK.

FOR MY HUSBAND, EDDY McGRIGOR,
GREAT-GREAT-NEPHEW OF MARIA HARGOOD
AND FOR OUR GRAND-DAUGHTER, SARAH
McGRIGOR, BORN ON 21 OCTOBER 1989,
'TRAFALGAR DAY'.

CONTENTS

ACKNOWLEDGEMENTS

My most sincere thanks to all those who have helped me with the writing and production of this book:-

In particular to:

Mr John Wyllie for permission to reprint his grandfather's picture on the cover of this book

Rear-Admiral C.H Layman, DSO, LVO

Commander Robert Manson

Mr Michael Shortall of Ballylorcan

Mr Tony Dalton

Mrs Joy Dunner

Brigadier Henry Wilson, Publishing Manager, Pen & Sword

Mr Tom Hartman, meticulous editor of the book

Mrs Barbara Bramall of Pen & Sword

Miss Hannah Crowdie, curator of the Worthing Museum Art Gallery

Mr David Taylor, of the Picture Gallery, National Maritime Museum, Greenwich

Mr Colin Starkey of the above

Mr Roy Eason of the above

Mr Brian Tynne, Curator of Hydrography of N.M.M.

Mr Malcolm Bruce of Dalmally, for photocopying

Mr Frank Walton of Oban

Mrs Janet Summerlin

My daughter Mrs Kirsty MacLaren for proof-reading

Miss Amabel Barraclough, my grand-daughter, for proof-reading and much help with the index.

My husband Sir Charles McGrigor, for his ever unfailing help

GLOSSARY

The following list of nautical terms, mainly concerned with sailing ships in the 18th –19th centuries, may be of help to the reader.

Bolt Rope : A rope sewn round the edge of a sail to keep the canvas from fraying.

Bower Anchor : One of the two longest anchors on either bow. They were kept ready for letting go at all times, in case of emergency.

Break : A rise or fall in the level of the deck.

Cable Length : A measure of distance at sea –200 yards (187 metres).

Close-hauled : In a square-rigged ship when the sails are set as near to the fore-and-aft line as possible in order to gain the maximum advantage of the wind coming over the bow.

Fathom : Measure of the depth of water. One fathom is equal to 1.8256 metres.

Fish : A piece of wood used to strengthen a damaged mast, like a splint.

Fly : The part of a flag furthest from the staff.

Galley : In this case, the ship's kitchen.

Guns : Ships were classified by the number of guns they carried, hence *Triumph* -74, meaning that she was armed with 74 guns. **Ships of the line** those deemed sufficiently well armed to lie in the **line of battle**, usually carried 50 or more guns, but this depended on the strength of the enemy.

Heave the log : A wooden board, called the "log", was "heaved" from the stern of the vessel, attached to a log-line, which was measured out in spaces marked by "knots". In this way the distance travelled could be calculated.

Jib-Boom : A continuation of the bowsprit, the large spar projecting from the bow of a sailing ship.

Key (Cay) : A small islet in the West Indies.

Lee : The side of a ship which is away from the wind.

Mizen or **Mizzen** : The aftermost mast of a square-rigged sailing ship.

Orlop Deck : The lowest deck in a ship.

Pendant (pronounced and often written **Pennant**) : A narrow tapering flag used for signalling. The **Broad Pendant**, which was swallow-tailed, was the distinguishing flag of a commadore.

Pollacre : A ship or brig found only in the Mediterranean with an unusual combination of lateen and square-rigged sails.

Poop : The aftermast deck, raised above the **Quarterdeck.** The poop light, therefore, indicated the aft end of the vessel.

Quarterdeck : The upper deck of a sailing ship abaft the mainmast, from which she was commanded by the Captain.

Slings : Ropes or chains used to hoist any heavy article.

Staysail : A triangual free-and-aft sail extended on a stay, which is part of the rigging supporting a mast.

Studdingsail (pronounced **stunsal**) : A sail set in fine weather, with the wind abaft the beam, outside the square sails.

Warp : To warp a ship is to move it by means of an anchor or by manpower from one place to another when in harbour.

Wear : To bring a ship on to the opposite tack by bringing the wind around the stern, as opposed to tackup, when the wind is brought round the bow.

INTRODUCTION

Queen Adelaide, wife and then widow of King William IV, was renowned for her kindness of heart. With no surviving children of her own, she yet lavished attention upon her husband's numerous illegitimate offspring who hung around the court. Coming from Germany, where she had been raised in the strict regime of a minor court, she nonetheless had a warmth of character which attracted a quick response. Foremost amongst her many acquaintances were Admiral Sir William Hargood, a former shipmate of her husband, and his wife Maria, with whom she developed a special rapport.

King William was not the easiest man to live with. He had an irascible temper and easily grew bored. His happiest years were in the Navy in which, having joined as a midshipman of sixteen, he ended up as Lord High Admiral of England. 'Sailor Bill' was in his element at sea. Essentially a man's man, he felt himself at home in a ship. His more endearing qualities included a capacity for both making and keeping friends. In particular he remained in constant touch with those with whom as a young man he had served at sea. Horatio Nelson was one, William Hargood another.

King William died in 1837 and Admiral William two years later, in 1839. Afterwards their widows continued to correspond. It may have been at Queen Adelaide's suggestion that Maria Hargood commissioned Joseph Allen, a naval historian of the time, to write the biography of her husband, who, even by the standards of those days of high adventure, had led a remarkable life. The book, entitled 'A Memoir of Admiral Sir William Hargood, G.C.B., G.C.H', beautifully bound and embossed with gold, duly appeared in 1841. The title page informs us that it was printed in Greenwich, by Henry S. Richardson 'for private circulation only'.

The dedication to Queen Adelaide explains that it describes the life of Admiral Sir William Hargood 'who served as Lieutenant of the *Pegasus* and *Andromeda* when commanded by his late lamented Majesty, King William IV'.

Allen, in his preface, pays tribute to 'Thomas Freeman Jessep, the late Admiral's secretary, who also served under him in the *Northumberland*; and also to Vice-Admiral Sir Jaheel Brenton, Colonel Owen, Captains Gordon Falcon, Sir George Westphal, Connolly, and to many other officers who, at different times, served under the Admiral's command.'

The acknowledgements prove that he wrote from first-hand accounts. Thus, I have indented the quotes from Allen's book. I hope that, in so doing, I have given both a clearer explanation of the events which he describes, as well as an easier read.

Maria Hargood, a daughter of the banker Thomas Somers Cocks, was my husband's great-great aunt, this being why we have a copy of the biography that she commissioned Joseph Allen to write. We also have mementos of the admiral, including the barometer, still in working order, on which he saw the pressure plunge, before his by then unmanageable ship met the full force of a storm of hurricane strength.

A picture of the *Belleisle* on the evening of Trafalgar shows her as a hulk, her masts shot away to a single stump on which a tattered Union Jack flies in defiance of defeat. Behind the wreck lies the *Victory* on which, some two hours earlier, Nelson had died from the bullet fired by a sniper on the French *Redoubtable*. Still farther in the background flames from the French *Achille* shoot upwards to the sky. The fire, started by sparks from the muskets of the sharp-shooters, which set her rigging alight, is out of control. She is about to explode. Most of her crew have jumped overboard and British sailors are risking their own lives in the ship's boats, as they pull their enemies from the sea.

The picture gives a vivid visual impression of the horrors of war in wooden ships. It also imparts an idea of the courage and compassion of the combatants involved. Tough sailors, many pressed from the prisons, wept at the death of Nelson. Their story is tied inevitably to that of the captains of Trafalgar, acclaimed as heroes to this day.

The adventures of William Hargood are not unique. Others endured imprisonment from which, unlike him, they did not escape with their lives. Danger on land and sea was commonplace, particularly in times of war. The threat of incurable and highly contagious disease was ever-present, especially in tropical climates, where, as the British Empire expanded, the ships of her navy inevitably were sent.

Hargood's story is nonetheless of interest in that it sheds light on the perilous and often horrific conditions that the men of what we now call 'Nelson's Navy' endured. Also it gives an insight into the character of a little man, who, without the benefit of social status, so necessary to promotion in those times, reached a high rank in his profession through his own integrity and skill.

John Masefield tells us that the competence and contentment of a ship's crew depended largely on the captain. Hargood's ships were happy ones, with the notable exception of the *Leopard*, but even then the mutineers who seized her made sure he came to no harm. Despite his lack of inches, his men looked up to him in a figurative way. Lieutenant Nicolas, remembering Trafalgar, described how, in the awful silence which prevailed on board the *Belleisle* before a shot could be fired, the commanding voice of Captain Hargood, 'that gallant little man', directed the quartermaster at the wheel.

Later, in the aftermath of the battle, in his cabin, which miraculously survived intact, Hargood restored the morale of his own men and of a Spanish captain who had been taken prisoner by courteously offering them tea. Even as they were drinking it, thankfully easing parched throats, news came that Nelson was dead. The Spanish captain, whose own admiral Don Ignacio de Alava, was lying unconscious in his flag-ship, shared in their devastating grief.

Moments like this make history. Thus the story of William Hargood, who lived through and saw it all, deserves, I believe, to be told. The book written by Joseph Allen, published in 1841, is typical of the stilted style of authors of his time. In addition it fails in most instances to describe not only the places but the people with whom Hargood was involved.

I have, for this reason, introduced both changes and additions to the text. Hopefully, in doing so I have made it easier for events, locations and characters to spring to the mind's eye. Hargood, a man of few words, who hated all forms of sycophancy, would, I hope, have approved!

A SAILOR AT THE AGE OF TEN

Hezekiah Hargood Esq was an independent gentleman
residing on Blackheath, in the county of Kent. He had nine
children, some of whom were daughters. The eldest son was
bred to the bar, and died in London; the others to different
professions. William, the youngest son, was born on the 6th
May, 1762.

So wrote Joseph Allen, commissioned biographer of the last-named
youngest son.

He adds that Hezekiah was of good social standing despite a
bygone scandal which had thrown the family into disgrace. This had
happened when his grandfather, descended from the Earl of
Harcourt, had eloped with a ward in chancery and been banished
from the country. However, when eventually pardoned, his
descendants, now calling themselves Hargood, having applied to
the Herald's office, were allowed to bear the Harcourt arms.

As a country gentleman Hezekiah had an income of his own.
Nonetheless, with a wife and nine children to support, he must have
struggled to find his sons employment let alone provide dowries for
his girls.

However, friends of influence in the navy came to his aid and
William was sent to join the service as a little boy of ten.

Leaving home must have been an ordeal. His mother and sisters
were doubtless in tears. But boys did not cry and the little figure, his
few possessions in a tin sea chest, probably showed the courage for
which he was later famed.

Uniform for military officers, introduced in 1748, had laid down
that 'Persons acting as Midshipmen should likewise have a uniform

cloathing in order to distinguish their Class to be in the Rank of Gentlemen'. The white patch or 'turnback' on the midshipman's collar appears to have been introduced at this time. Certainly, the regulations in 1787 mention 'a stand up collar with small white turn back *as before*'. The patch was known to generations as a midshipman's 'weekly account', and by the midshipmen themselves as 'the mark of the beast'.[1]*

Going by contemporary illustrations, the young William Hargood would therefore have set out on his great adventure decked out in a swallowtail coat, with the aforementioned white patch on the turnback of the collar. Beneath he would have worn a waistcoat above knee breeches, silk stockings and pumps, or at least flat-heeled shoes which would not mark the deck. Once on board he would have worn a short jacket, known for obvious reasons as a 'bum freezer', for everyday wear on the ship.

Although by today's standards it seems almost inhuman to send a little boy of ten to sea, it was the done thing at the time. The idea was that he would then get the necessary education that the naval officer, which he hoped to become, would need. This education, too often very sketchy, was to be acquired in large ships only, to which a schoolmaster was appointed by the Admiralty.

Another reason for sending boys to face the hardships, the severe discipline and the dangers of life on a warship was to give them a head start in their profession. It was not unusual for young men to hold lieutenant's commissions at the age of sixteen, while many post captains had not reached their twentieth year. The navy, like the empire, was expanding. The administration of the East India Company had just been passed by Lord North's government in the Regulation Act of 1773. Trade in the Far East was booming, but piracy was rife. The merchant ships needed protection and the need for naval escorts was putting a strain on the navy which brought a great increase in shipbuilding and also subsequent advancement in the service for ambitious young men.

Young William, small as he was for his age, nonetheless proved himself industrious and quick to learn. He was eleven when he joined the *Triumph*, 74, bearing the broad pendant of Commodore Maurice Suckling, in the River Medway. Suckling, although now

* See notes on p. 183.

2

largely remembered as the maternal uncle of Horatio Nelson, had himself had a notable career. A lieutenant by the time he was twenty-two, he had been in command of the battleship *Dreadnought*, when he was only thirty-two, at the beginning of the Seven Years War. Most famously, on 21 October 1757, the *Dreadnought*, together with three other British battleships, had defeated a larger French squadron. This was the reason why Nelson, when heading into battle in the *Victory* exactly forty-eight years later, told his officers that the 21st of October had always been thought 'a fortunate day' day by his family.

In 1770, when made captain of the battleship *Raisonable*, Suckling had taken his sister's boy to sea. Horatio was then only twelve and so delicate that his uncle, a kind-hearted man, had exclaimed, 'What has poor little Horace done that he should be sent to sea?' Nonetheless, Horace, as he was known to his family, insisted and got his way. And so the legend of his life began.

Captain Suckling had in fact been removed to the *Triumph* by the time that little William Hargood joined his ship. By this time his nephew, Horatio, four years older than William, had left to join a merchantman. Thus it was not until later, when both were serving on the *Bristol* in 1799, that Hargood made the acquaintance of the then lieutenant who he later called his 'oldest friend'.

Hargood, like Nelson, joined the ship as a 'first-class volunteer', the name given to the 'youngsters' who could not become midshipmen until they were fifteen. They were also called 'Captain's Boys', thanks to being related to the captain – he often took his sons to sea – or because an acquaintance, or someone with influence, had persuaded him to take them aboard.

These lads, known on the ship as 'the young gentlemen', lived under the care of the gunner who kept an eye on their health. He also saw to it that their clothes were washed either on board or by one of the washerwomen who lived in every port. In some ships the gunner's wife, who sailed with him, washed and mended their garments. After they had been climbing the rigging, their jackets, breeches and stockings were usually streaked with strong-smelling tar.

All the midshipmen slept on the orlop deck in the lower regions of the ship directly above the hold. The 'youngsters' slung their hammocks in the gun room, while the fully fledged midshipmen (some of whom were middle-aged) were crowded into the cockpit.

Above them on the lower gun deck the seamen swung in hammocks, which the regulations dictated must be no more than fourteen inches apart. This, however, was not quite as uncomfortable as it sounds, because men on alternate watches usually slept side by side. Thus when the starboard watch took up their stations at 8 p.m. the men of the larboard watch had empty hammocks beside them. As the ship's bell was sounded at midnight, the boatswain's mates yelled, 'Larboard watch! Rouse out there you sleepers.' The men of the starboard watch then had a bare four hours of rest until, at four o'clock in the morning, they had to start sanding, brushing and holy-stoning the decks.

The midshipmen, if not on a night watch, were roused at seven in the morning. Their hammocks were stowed for them by the 'hammock man', an old sailor who would do this and other tasks, such as sometimes washing their shirts, in return for a weekly glass of grog. The midshipmen, however, were responsible for seeing that the sailors stacked their hammocks to the bulwarks of the decks. The straw mattresses, dubbed a 'donkey's breakfast', and two blankets, rolled up and lashed like sausages, acted as padding against splinters during a battle when cannon balls crashed against the hull.

The decks were already spotless before the crew was piped down to breakfast at eight o'clock. This meal consisted largely of oatmeal, cooked together with the weevils which usually lived in it and which was known as 'burgoo' Cocoa, or a brew called 'Scotch coffee' – water in which ships' biscuits, first roasted in the oven, had been soaked and sugar added - were at least hot drinks. In cold weather men came down from the topmasts frozen almost beyond words, while the hands of those working on deck were raw and bleeding from heaving on ice-covered ropes.

At exactly half-past nine on a weekday (on Sunday it was ten o'clock) the captain inspected the ship. The sailors, clean-shaven and with their pigtails plaited, stood to attention while he examined every corner for dirt and every shroud, sail and halyard for signs of wear and tear.

The 'youngsters' were spared this ritual, being hard at their lessons from nine to twelve. The schoolmaster was usually the chaplain – often tormented by his pupils with ingenious practical jokes – although in some smaller ships the captain taught them himself. The teacher, whoever he was, had to pass an examination in navigation before the authorities at Trinity House appointed him to the post. His salary was between £2 and £2 8s a month, with a bounty of £5 for each midshipman in his class. The boys were taught in trigonometry and nautical astronomy, the basis of the science of navigation so vital to men at sea. At noon, carrying their quadrants, they trooped up to the deck to check the ship's position from the sun. No boy was allowed his dinner until he got it right![2]

In addition to this, the lads had to be able to recognize and memorize the meaning of all the signals conveyed on the captain's orders by flags run up and down the mast. Signals had at first been sent by lanterns hung at various heights on the mast. The first unofficial book of signals was only produced in 1689. A printed book followed in 1714, which in turn was replaced by a revised version in 1746. This was probably the one that Hargood first used. It contained the Articles of War and the regulations for the 'Duty of Every Officer in his Majesty's Sea-Service', together with the 'Flags of all Nations', beautifully painted by hand. Flags, set out along the tops of pages, were numbered, the signals conveyed by their position being listed below. The Red Ensign, signal 9, for instance, when flown from the masthead signified a summons 'to speak with the Admiral'. But hoisted above the mizen shrouds it meant that 'the Admiral wishes to make contact with all masters of merchant ships'.

Lessons once over, it was time for what the majority on board considered to be the most important moment of the day – namely the first issue of the 'Royal Navy's liquid happiness' – beer, wine or rum. A seaman was allowed a daily ration of a gallon of rather weak beer, or, when this was finished, a pint of wine. Finally, on a long cruise, when all else had run dry, there was always the favourite tipple of a gill of pure rum mixed with three gills of water. The midshipmen were limited to the maximum of a half ration until they were at least fifteen.

Then it was down for dinner, the main meal of the day.

The sailors messed in groups of their own choice. Gathering round tables, let down from the ceiling of the lower deck between the guns, they perched themselves on chests and kitbags, whatever they could find. Each mess had a steward, who, having collected the provisions from the stores, took them along to the galley to be cooked.

The food, unwholesome from the start, became increasingly revolting the longer the ship stayed at sea. In Scotland farmers were making fortunes from the sale of small Highland cattle, driven to the markets from the hills. The trade had begun to boom in the mid-eighteenth century when, as the wars with European countries had begun, the government bought huge quantities of meat to feed the fighting men. There was of course no refrigeration, but, salted down in tubs, it could keep for several years.

Unfortunately, due to economy, the old meat had to be eaten first. Tough, and full of bone and gristle, it was soaked in the ship's often filthy water for only twenty-four hours and came out still glistening with particles of salt. Then, as John Masefield claimed, 'It needed a magician rather than a cook to make it edible.'[3] Some of the hardest lumps, which were uneatable, were carved by the sailors with their penknives into boxes and other trinkets which they sold when they went ashore. Reputedly, when polished they took on a very good shine. Tuesdays and Saturdays were salt-beef days. Sundays and Thursdays were pork. On Mondays, Wednesdays and Fridays no meat was issued, but the cooks, given a few raisins, added them to flour and lard to concoct the sailor's favourite, plum duff.

Tea, at about five o'clock, usually consisted of ship's biscuit and cheese washed down with the second issue of whatever drink was on board. This was the last meal of the day and the boys, who naturally were always hungry, were up to all sorts of tricks to get food. 'Cutting out' expeditions, usually highly organized, resulted in midnight feasts. The midshipmen of the night watches would contrive to get into the steward's pantry, and sometimes even into the wardroom pantry, and snaffle what they could find. Sometimes it was a leg or two of chicken and, if they were lucky, even some wine.

'We never regarded this as dishonesty,' wrote Admiral John Moresby in his memoirs. 'It was a buccaneering expedition, which brought a certain amount of honour and glory to its successful exponents.'[4]

Hard though it was for those little boys who went to sea, the 'youngsters' in a ship with good officers were to a certain extent shielded from the worst of the coarseness and cruelty of life aboard a ship of the Royal Navy. They ate by themselves in the gunroom, catered for by the gunner, who, when possible, bought them treats such as fruit and tea, for which they paid themselves. Midshipmen, especially the 'Captain's boys', had to have some private means. The money was paid directly to the Captain, who doled out an allowance, to prevent extravagance, of not more than fifteen shillings a week.

A man-of-war like the *Triumph* was a world unto itself, over which the Captain ruled supreme. None dared to challenge his authority. The punishment for striking him, or indeed any of the officers, was death. Below him, in order of seniority, came the lieutenants. On a ship of 74 guns like the *Triumph* there would probably have been three or four. The first lieutenant was the Captain's mouthpiece, issuing his orders to the crew.

Next in rank to the lieutenants was the master, the man in charge of the sailing of the ship, and of the setting, trimming and repair of the sails. Under the Captain's orders he conducted the ship from port to port. Before leaving harbour he had to supervise the stowage of both ballast and cargo in the hold, making sure that there was enough wood and coal for the galley fires, and sufficient barrels of water in the hold to last the voyage. In addition, he had sole charge of the spirit room where a naked light could never be carried lest the fumes of the spirits should catch fire.

Most importantly, each day at noon he had to find the ship's position by a process of mathematics and the firmaments in the sky. The master's mates, who assisted him, had to heave the log every hour, or half hour, and to keep the log-book up to date.

The boatswain, most important of the warrant officers, had his own cabin in the fore cockpit. Usually an old sailor, he had charge of the 'boats, sails, rigging, colours, anchors, cables and cordage'.[5] In his uniform of a blue cloth coat and white or blue trousers, and his low, glazed tophat embellished with a cockade, he made a distinctive figure. A whistle, hanging on a silver chain round his neck, symbolized his office. Upon an officer giving an order he blew it, before shouting the instructions down the hatchway. His mates then repeated them until the bawling was echoing round the ship.

The boatswain was in charge of the ship's boats when on board. In calm weather one was lowered once a day so that he could be rowed round the vessel to inspect her hull. In battle he commanded the forecastle and his privileges included that of 'piping the side' when the Captain came aboard.[6]

The boatswain's mates, writes Masefield, 'were chosen from the very best seamen on board. They were the leaders, or drivers of the crew, and generally the finest men in the fleet.' Sailors were kept up to scratch with swipes from their knotted ropes. Moreover, they had to obey the Captain by flogging miscreants on his orders.

The purser, who ranked with the boatswain, was often a less

worthy character. He it was who examined the food that came on board. Dates chalked on casks could be altered, giving him, and dishonest purveyors, a chance of feathering their nests. From the purser's room on the orlop deck he served out provisions to the cooks of the messes, having first weighed each item with care. The purser also kept the slop books, 'slops' being the sailor's word for the clothing and bedding issued by the naval storekeepers to every ship in the fleet. Most importantly, he kept the ship's muster roll, from which the whole crew was counted, immediately after an action, or otherwise every ten days.

The gunner, of equal rank to the purser (both wore the same uniform as the boatswain), was in total charge of the guns and ammunition on the ship. His duties, and those of his crew in the course of an action, are later described. Equally important was the carpenter, the man whose expertise secured the safety of everyone on board a wooden ship.

The quartermaster, usually an old hand like the boatswain, in addition to keeping a check on both equipment and provisions, kept the time. The ship's bell was struck at each half-hour. The sail-maker, with a gang of men assisting, had a busy time of it, mending and patching after a gale or an action, when the canvas had been torn to shreds. The master-at-arms, the ship's policeman, was responsible for posting sentinels if a company of marines was not aboard. One stood before the door of the galley within which laboured the cook. This worthy, last but by no means the least important of the warrant officers, although largely derided for his efforts, did at least endeavour to keep the men alive.

Some of the crew were volunteers but many were rounded up by press gangs or released from jail to serve on ships. The latter, frequently imprisoned for minor offences such as stealing a sheep, when once accustomed to discipline, often became good hands at sea.

Seamen coming aboard were allocated to their positions by the first lieutenant. First, he selected the older and more experienced to work on the forecastle. The younger and most athletic became topmen on one of the three masts, fore, main and mizzen. Climbing the rigging was perilous: a moment's lack of concentration was enough to cause a fatal fall. Wooden platforms, attached to the masts, were called the tops. Above them the topmasts rose to the cross-trees where lookouts perched precariously in ever constant watch. Those less able and active handled the mainsail and lower sails of the ship

The largest section of the crew, however, known as the waisters, worked, as their name implies, in the middle of the ship. Hauling on the mainsheets and scrubbing the decks, their tasks also included mucking out and feeding the cattle, sheep and pigs that a battleship carried in an enclosure termed the 'manger', specifically for fresh food. The butcher was among the many individuals in what could truly be called 'a motley crew'. At the bottom of the heap were the boys, the powder boys who carried ammunition to the guns, and the loblolly boys who helped the surgeon and the fifers, usually the smallest of all. Most of these children had been taken from orphanages or else picked up homeless from the street.

The midshipmen, by and large, were used as 'dog's bodies' by the first lieutenant. As potential officers they had to learn all the working of a ship. One of them was always stationed in each top when sails were being furled, in order to cheer up the men to do their job as quickly and efficiently as was possible. The efficiency of a battleship depended to a great extent on the skill and speed of the sailors in raising and lowering the sails.

The numerous tasks allotted to the midshipmen included the supervision of the hoisting aboard of stores. More pleasant and more exciting was an order to command the crew of one of the of the ship's boats. This meant going ashore to fetch water, or taking messages to other ships in the fleet. Hardest of all, at least for the 'youngsters', were the night watches of four hours at a time. Somehow they had to keep awake on the quarterdeck, 'to heave the log and mark the board' and run errands for the officer on watch.

Promotion within the Navy, as in the Army, in the late 18th century, depended largely upon family connections. Commodore Suckling, a sound if not a brilliant man, had married the daughter of the first Lord Walpole, who saw to it that his son-in-law's career advanced. Thus, when appointed to the prime position of Controller of the Navy Board, he hauled down his pendant on 25 December 1773 and exchanged his cabin on the *Triumph* for the spacious rooms of Somerset House in its splendid surroundings in the Strand.

Commodore Suckling was succeeded in command of the ship by Captain the Hon George Falconer, who continued to command her until 25 January 1775. William Hargood thus remained aboard her until he was almost thirteen.

The *Triumph* being laid up, Captain Falconer removed into the *Mars*, 50, which was fitting for service at Woolwich. It then being the custom for members of the crew to move with their captains, young William Hargood followed him into that ship. He did not stay long, however, for Captain the Hon George Keith Elphinstone, having commissioned the *Romney*, 50, for the flag of Rear-Admiral Robert Duff, undertook the charge of the still youthful midshipman, and the *Romney* was the first ship in which he braved the perils of the ocean.

The *Romney* was fitting for sea at Deptford, when, on 11 March 1775 William Hargood joined her. On 6 April the ship left her moorings at Deptford and proceeded down river as far as Long Beach. Here she remained to complete her crew and take her guns on board. She sailed from thence in May and on the 24th arrived at Spithead. On the 26th Rear-Admiral Duff hoisted his flag in her and proceeded to Plymouth, but finally left England for Newfoundland on 10 June.

On her passage out the *Romney* was joined by the *Martin* sloop, and, after a pleasant voyage both ships arrived at St John's.

THE *BRISTOL*: INTRODUCTION TO WAR

A ship carrying fifty guns, as did the *Romney*, was reckoned a fourth-rate warship. As such she would have carried about 650 men, who included about 120 marines. These men, in their red jackets, pipe-clayed trousers and hats with a smart cockade, slept and messed apart from the sailors, who thought themselves superior to the men of the 'sea regiment', as marines originally were named.

The marines stood sentry outside the captain's cabin, magazine hatchways and in various other parts of the ship which, when the cooks were working, included the galley door! In action they were sharpshooters, trained to pick off the men in the rigging of the enemy' ships. Their prime duty however, was to captain the naval gun-crews which fired the mighty iron-cast cannons with such deadly accuracy and speed.

By the time he arrived in Newfoundland William Hargood had become familiar with gun practise which at sea was an almost daily event. The swiftness and precision of running out the cannons, loading, firing and re-loading, was often a main factor in deciding between victory and defeat.

The guns were kept in readiness, a cartridge rammed up the barrel above one, sometimes two, or even three iron balls. Only the powder was added at the last minute before firing, so that it would not get damp. The gun crews comprised four men, a captain of marines, a sponger, a boarder armed with a cutlass, and a fireman with a bucket who was ready to douse a flame immediately, should a spark set anything on board alight. Beside them a ship's boy stood ready to dash for powder from the magazine.

Each group of guns, usually four in number, was in charge of a midshipman, or in some cases a master's mate. Gun practice, known as 'beating to quarters', was essential, so that in an emergency each of the bare-footed sailors ran almost automatically to his allotted place.

On the Captain's order 'Cast free your gun' the men loosed the guns from the tackles which held them securely to the side of the ship. A cannon breaking loose to crash about the deck was feared almost as much as fire in a wooden ship. The captain of marines, once his gun was levelled and run out, first rammed his priming-iron down the touch-hole to pierce the flannel cartridge lying within the barrel, before pouring powder from his horn into the vent and on to the pan. The sponger, keeping his hand over the powder to stop it blowing away, then turned to one side to puff on the slow match pulled from a tinder box. The match was banged down on to the priming by the marine. There was a hissing, a flash and an ear-splitting roar as the iron shot burst from the muzzle. The noise, the stench of cordite and the smoke in the confined space of the gun decks, exciting as it was to a boy, must at times have been terrifying, especially if the sea was rough.

As soon as the lookouts saw the sails of a possible enemy rising above the horizon action stations were called. The drummer of the marines beat the summons, short and sharp, to the tune 'Hearts of Oak'. Every man of the crew knew and had memorized his own particular tasks. The carpenter and his mates knocked the wooden bulkheads, dividing the officer's cabins, from their grooves and men carried them down to the holds. Likewise the captain's furniture was removed, or in a sudden emergency actually heaved overboard. So too went the chicken coops and the cows and sheep in the manger. Only the pigs, being solid and slow, were generally allowed to remain.

On the lower decks men from each mess stowed away the sea-chests, kitbags and crockery. Above, on the masts, the topmen secured the sail sheets and dragged up some coils of rope and spars with which to make running repairs. Buckets of water were hauled aloft and poured over the sails to prevent them from catching alight, while nets were stretched below to catch debris falling from above.

Fire was an ever-present fear in a combustible wooden ship. To prevent it, hoses were laid along every deck and wet sand sprinkled on the planking: the latter precaution being taken to stop men slipping in blood.

While those appointed to these tasks worked swiftly, others

prepared the guns. The powder- boys pelted up with cartridges from the magazine, covering them with their coats to keep them dry. The gun-captains hung up their powder-horns and stuck priming-irons into their belts. The marines, who were not assigned to the gun crews, took up their station on the top deck ready to pick off the men on the enemy's rigging with their muskets as soon as they came within range. Such was the efficiency of a well-run ship, carrying a full complement of hands, that it took only four or five minutes to clear the decks for action.

The *Romney* stayed only a short time on the coast of Newfoundland. The savage winds and frequent snow-storms made it unwise to winter there. As it was, when she sailed from St John's harbour on 27 October 1775 she ran into a severe gale off the banks of Nova Scotia. The ship was damaged to the point where she was nearly wrecked. Fortunately, however, the wind was from the west. She was put before it and hurtled across the Atlantic, reaching Spithead on 13 November after a voyage of only seventeen days.

On 19 November Rear-Admiral Duff struck his flag and the following month William Hargood moved into the *Bristol*, then recently commissioned for Commodore Sir Peter Parker. The commodore, being an old friend of William's father, had promised to take the young midshipman under his special care.

The amazing efficiency of the shipyards in England, then working to the limit of their ability, is proved by the fact that the *Bristol*, a 50-gun ship, commissioned on the stocks at Sheerness by Captain John Morris only early in October, was launched on the 25th of the same month.

So urgent was the demand for vessels in the emergency caused by the war in America that the ship was rigged and ready for sea by the 14 December. [This was a prodigious feat, even bearing in mind that at this time ships were often rigged before launching.] Once in the water the *Bristol* sailed for Spithead where, on the 19th, Sir Peter Parker hoisted his broad pendant.

The American War of Independence had begun. The British Navy at this point had 375 ships of which 58 were ships of the line and 198 frigates, the rest being in reserve. Nonetheless, despite the strength of the fleet, it could not subdue the insurgents as is proved by contemporary reports.

From these it can be seen that the British government, still headed by Lord North, had greatly underestimated both the strength and the patriotic fervour of the American rebels. In particular the power and influence of George Washington had been largely unrecognised for its worth. Thus, for both of these reasons, the British forces, undermanned and in many cases ill equipped, were defeated to the amazement of the politicians for whom an over-riding victory had seemed a foregone conclusion.

Sir Peter Parker, an old and greatly experienced officer, was given the command of a squadron to be sent to South Carolina where the men of the Confederate army, having overthrown the Loyalists, were holding out in defiance of the expected arrival of an army sent from Britain to uphold their enemies.

The *Bristol* sailed from Spithead on the 29th December 1775 in company with the *Actaeon, Deal Castle,* and *Thunder Bomb.,* and proceeded to Cork, at which place a fleet of thirty transports laden with military stores, and having on board a large body of troops under the command of Earl Cornwallis, was collected, destined for an attack on Charleston, South Carolina.

A large group of people from Scotland, who included the heroine Flora MacDonald – saviour of Bonny Prince Charlie - and her family from Skye, had recently settled in North Carolina. They had arrived there almost as the American colonists, infuriated by the taxation imposed by the British Government, in which they themselves had no representation, were uniting in rebellion against what they believed to be an unjust law. The Governor of North Carolina, Josiah Martin, who had served as a regular soldier in the British army, had sent an urgent appeal to the British Government asking for ships and soldiers to be sent to support the Loyalists, now threatened with loss of life and land. The force commanded by Major-General William Howe, who replaced Lord Cornwallis, almost as the ships set sail, was thus sent to their aid.

The *Bristol* and a squadron consisting of the *Active, Actaeon, Solebay,* and *Carcass,* with the above-mentioned transports, finally left Cork on the 12th February 1776; and, after encountering a heavy gale of wind, in which many of the transports parted company, reached Cape Fear, on the 5th April,

14

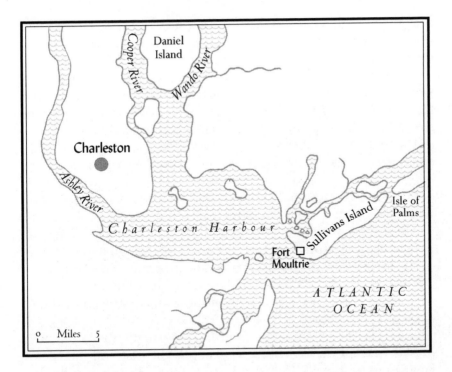

where they were soon afterwards joined by most of the missing transports.

Lieutenant-General Clinton, with a body of land forces, here joined, and took command of the expedition, the preparations of which being completed, the whole fleet of forty-nine sail departed on the 1st of June.

On 4 June the *Bristol* anchored off Charleston.

Charleston, the principal city of South Carolina, stands on a point of land formed by the confluence of the Ashley and Cooper rivers which converge immediately below the city to form a spacious harbour which communicates with the ocean just below Sullivan's island. The situation of Charleston is naturally very strong. The fort now erected on the southern part of Sullivan's Island is termed Fort Moultrie. The rise and fall of the tide is between six and seven feet.

The city, first colonized in 1670, had survived many disasters, including hurricanes and epidemics. An earthquake in 1697 had

15

been followed in the next year by a fire which had wiped out a third of the colony. Now, as the English fleet approached, the colonists, terrified but defiant, mustered to repel attack. Hurriedly they constructed a redoubt to strengthen Fort Moultrie as British ships were seen off the harbour mouth. Meanwhile the Americans, under the command of Major-General Lee, were making every effort to strengthen their position and were daily increasing in number.

The *Bristol* lay at anchor for two days while soundings were made and buoys put in place to guide the ship over the harbour bar.

It was, however, found impracticable, from the shallowness of the water, for [her] to cross the bar with her guns on board. These were, therefore, got out and put on board a transport. Finally on the 10th her crew succeeded in getting her over the bar to anchor with the frigates and transports in Five Fathom Hole, where she again took on board her guns. On the 16th an American privateer was driven on shore and destroyed by the boats of the *Bristol*.

By this time all the British troops had disembarked on the Isle of Palms[1] and encamped. This island, just to the north-east of Sullivan's Island, also lies parallel to the coast. The two are separated by a narrow channel, reputedly easy to cross.

On the strength of intelligence brought to them by their scouts, General Clinton and Sir Peter Parker, believing that Fort Moultrie on Sullivan's Island was in a decrepit state, decided that an attempt should be made upon it forthwith.

It is most probable that their plans would have succeeded had it not been for an unforeseen occurrence which threw the whole weight of the attack on the squadron. The troops were to have forded the passage separating the Isle of Palms from Sullivan's Island, which had been sounded and the depth reported to be not more than eighteen inches at low water. However, when the men attempted to cross the channel the water was found to be over seven feet in depth. Had the soldiers even attempted to cross it, they would undoubtedly have been drowned. Later, an American writer was to explain that the fluctuation in the depth of water between these two islands is influenced by the prevailing winds.

On the 25th [June] the squadron was increased by the arrival of the *Experiment*, of 50 guns, Captain Scott.

It then consisted of the following.

Gun ships

50 *Bristol*	Commodore Sir Peter Parker
	Captain John Morris
Experiment	Captain Scott.
28 *Solebay*	Captain John Symonds
Actaeon	Captain Christopher Atkins
Active	Captain William Williams
Syren	Captain Furneaux
20 *Sphynx*	Captain Anthony Hunt

Armed ships	*Ranger*	Captain Roger Willis.
	Friendship	Captain Charles Hope.
Bombs	*Thunder*	Captain James Reid.
	Carcass	Captain Thomas Dring.

On the 28th, the weather proving favourable, Sir Peter Parker at half-past nine made the signal to General Clinton, agreed upon to begin the attack. At ten o'clock the Commodore made the signal for the squadron to weigh and proceed towards Charleston. An hour and twenty minutes later, at twenty minutes past eleven, the batteries opened their fire upon the *Bristol* and *Active*, as these ships advanced to take up their stations.

The *Active* anchored off the east bastion, *Experiment* off the west bastion and part of the curtain, the *Solebay* off the west bastion, and the *Bristol* off the curtain, in seven fathoms water, within two cable lengths.

The remaining ships of the squadron, *Sphynx*, *Actaeon*, and *Syren*, were placed to the westward, to prevent fireships and other vessels from annoying the ships under the forts, to enfilade the works of the besieged as much as possible, and to cut off their retreat should they attempt to abandon the island. But these ships, in proceeding to take up the stations assigned to them, unfortunately ran foul of each other, and all three got ashore on a shoal called the Middle Ground. At half-past one the *Sphynx* and *Syren* got off, but the *Actaeon* remained immovable.

To this accident and the disappointment caused by the failure of the attempt to ford the passage by the troops may be attributed the ill success of the attack, for the besieged, having no other object to take their attention, were enabled to bend all their efforts against the ships under the batteries.

The *Bristol*, from her situation, suffered severely, especially on her upper deck, not a man upon it escaping; Sir Peter Parker was wounded in the head. The fire from the main and lower decks, however, was kept up with such vigour that by two o'clock the batteries ceased firing until half-past three.

The ebb now beginning to make, it was deemed advisable to drop the small bower anchor astern, so as to prevent the ship from swinging to the tide, which was accordingly done; but a little before four o'clock the forts reopened their fire, and a shot cutting the spring as well as the small bower cable, the ship swung to her best bower anchor.

In swinging she was exposed to a tremendous raking fire, the enemy's shot passing through and through her. Still the fire of the British ships was continued and with visible effect; the Americans were driven from their guns and many retired to the mainland, but were quickly replaced by fresh numbers. The batteries at times were deserted, and had it been possible for the army to have co-operated they must have been quickly possessed, but, from this want, fresh forces were emboldened to return.

After remaining under the forts for ten hours, and the night fast closing in, the Commodore found it necessary to retire. He accordingly made the signal for the ships to cut their cables and stand out of gun shot, which was effected by all without accident, except the *Active*, which ship tailed on shore. The boats of the squadron were immediately sent to her assistance, and she hauled off; but the *Actaeon*, being found immovable, was set on fire and destroyed.

The carnage on board the ships was very great, particularly in the *Bristol*; and Mr Hargood may be said to have been early initiated, and to have participated in an action, [which] though unsuccessful, [was] of no mean report. The loss on board his own ship amounted to forty killed, and Captain John Morris (mortally), Mr John Holland, master, and seventy-one men, wounded. Captain Morris lost his right arm, and received other wounds so severe, that he was obliged to be superseded, and died on board the *Pigot*, hospital ship, on the 5th July following. [The American Declaration of Independence had been made on the previous day.]

It is related of this gallant man that, upon finding his wound to be of a very dangerous nature, and one of his officers asking him if he had directions to give with respect to his family, he replied, 'None, as I leave them to the Providence of God, and the generosity of my country.'

How grateful his country proved to be is shown by the shabby behaviour of the British Government who allowed his widow, left to raise a young family on her own, a pension of a mere £100 a year.

Joseph Allen gives a short account of the life of James Nicoll Morris, son of the captain whose death he has just described, in an Appendix to his book. He states categorically that:

The son entered the navy at a very early age under his father's care, and was doomed, at the outset of his career, to undergo the most grievous misfortune which could have assailed him. His gallant father received such mortal injuries in the fatal attack upon the forts of Sullivan's Island, and it was found necessary to remove him to the *Pigot* hospital ship . . . where he died.

The *Bristol's* pay book, however, makes no mention of midshipman James Nicoll Morris. Therefore, it seems unlikely that he had to endure the trauma of seeing his father die from his wounds.

Allen, who does not refer to James Morris being on board, merely states:

In Captain Morris, Mr Hargood lost a kind friend and instructor, and the service of an excellent officer. With the son of this brave man . . . he long afterwards became connected by marriage, these two officers marrying sisters; and it is singular that both commanded line-of-battle ships at the renowned victory of Trafalgar, and were only two or three ships asunder.

The fact that Hargood, then just thirteen, survived the action unhurt indicates that Captain Morris, or Sir Peter Parker, the latter having promised his father to look after him, probably banished him from the main deck to comparative safety below. Nonetheless, he must have seen horribly mutilated men being carried down to the cockpit (normally the older midshipmen's mess) and have heard the screams and groans of agony as the surgeon hacked off limbs on the table on which the midshipmen normally ate their meals.

In addition to the loss of life and the many injuries to the crew, the *Bristol* itself, lying off Charleston, was found to be so badly damaged that she could not put out to sea:

> Her main and mizzen topmasts were shot away, and the mizzen mast fell over the side on the following day, before it could be secured. Two lower-deck guns, one on the main deck, and one on the quarterdeck were dismounted, and the ship generally disabled.

Captain Morris was succeeded in command by the first lieutenant, Toby Caulfield,[2] who, because of the casualties of the battle, found himself virtually without a crew. The situation was saved, however, by the masters and crews of the transports, of whom fifty volunteered to serve on the *Bristol* to replace the men who were too badly wounded to do any physical work.

3

PIRATES AND PLUNDERERS:
NORTH AMERICA TO THE WEST INDIES

Admiral Sir Peter Parker had a flair for detecting the qualities in his young officers which fitted them for promotion. Born in 1721, the son of Rear Admiral Sir Christopher Parker, he had gone to sea with his father at a very early age. Thus, in a literal sense, he was born and bred to the navy. A Post Captain when he was twenty-six, he had served throughout the Seven Years' War (1756-63). Most notably he had commanded the battleship *Buckingham* at the capture of the French-held island of Belle Ile off the coast of Brittany.* Knighted in 1772, he was a commodore on the America station before, on promotion to rear-admiral, he became Commander-in-Chief in Jamaica in 1778.

William Hargood, by this time, had served with him for over two years. Initially becoming his protégé on account of Parker's friendship with his father, he was soon to be recognized as his 'follower', a sure intimation of the Admiral's recognition of his ability, as Allen's narrative proves.

> After refitting his ships Sir Peter Parker sailed from Charleston on the 3rd August, and having re-embarked the troops in obedience to orders received from the Commander-in-Chief, proceeded to Sandy Hook and New York. On the 14th the *Bristol* arrived there, and found the *Eagle* bearing the flag of Vice-Admiral Lord Howe, who had arrived out from England to take command of the fleet.

Vice-Admiral Richard Howe was the second of the three sons of the second Viscount Howe who died in 1735. George, the eldest, who

---

* See footnote page 82.

21

succeeded him, became a Brigadier-General and was killed at the Battle of Ticonderoga in 1758. The title then devolved upon Richard, the second son, who, as has already mentioned, arrived in his flagship in New York in August 1776.

Legend has it that Admiral Howe had only agreed to accept his command on the given promise that he would be allowed to act as Royal Commissioner in an attempt to placate the colonies. He had already treated with Benjamin Franklin to try to work out peace proposals. He had also been thwarted in getting permission from Lord North's ministry to lead a peace delegation to the Colonies himself. A serious man, who seemed weighed down by responsibility, he was known in the Navy as 'Black Dick Howe', his skin having darkened from exposure to the weather during over thirty years at sea.

Richard Howe sailed in to North America where his brother William, three years younger than himself, had been in command of the land forces since the previous year. A less worthy character then Richard, he had already created a scandal by bringing his mistress, known as 'The Sultana', from Boston to New York. Nonetheless, he was renowned both for his courage and for his skill in organizing men and in planning military operations. Lord George Germain, Secretary of State for the American Colonies, said that no other officer was so well qualified to teach European soldiers how to fight 'from behind trees, walls or hedges'.

Both brothers are still remembered for the care and compassion that they showed for the men in their charge. William, called 'Gentleman Johnny' by his soldiers, had been horrified by the large number of men who had been killed in America during the previous year.

> On the arrival of this reinforcement, General Howe was enabled to commence operations for a descent upon Long Island. [The island, now connected by bridges, which lies east-north-east of New York.] On the 22nd August seventy-five flat boats manned from the fleet, together with eleven batteaux, two galleys, and the frigates *Rose*, *Phoenix* and *Greyhound*, were placed under the orders of Commodore Hotham, in order to cover the disembarkation of the troops in Gravesend Bay. Mr Hargood was, on this occasion, in command of one of the boats, and was, most probably, stationed in the division of Captain Caulfield.

The service was effected without loss, and with such expedition that before noon fifteen thousand men and forty pieces of cannon were landed on Long Island. The investment then succeeded rapidly; but during the various operations the flat boats were continually employed in annoying the enemy and in co-operating with the land forces. On these several occasions and during the whole of those important trans-actions, which ended in the retreat of Washington and complete reduction of the island, Mr Hargood participated fully. The value of the services rendered by the officers of the navy was such as to call forth the warmest praises from General Howe.

By this time Sir Peter Parker had removed his broad Commodore's pendant into the *Chatham*, 50, and thither Mr Hargood followed him. In December Sir Peter was sent with a squadron to attempt the reduction of Rhode Island. [An American state which lies 125 miles, or 200 kilometres, to the north-east of New York.]

On the 1st December the squadron, with the land forces of General Clinton [second in command to General Howe] departed, and on the 8th anchored in Weaver's Cove, Rhode Island, where the troops were disembarked without opposition. The enemy fled from their defences as the British advanced, and the island fell entirely into their possession. The great advantage of holding this place was that of its shutting out the numerous privateers who rendezvoused there, several of which were captured by the cruisers of the fleet.

The *Chatham* remained in Rhode Island harbour while it was occupied by the British, at which place, on the 22nd July, Sir Peter Parker hoisted his flag as Rear-Admiral. This service was not one of great activity, being principally confined to the blockade of the American naval force.

On the 25th December 1778 Sir Peter Parker returned to the *Bristol*. The ship, so badly damaged in Charleston Harbour, had been sent back across the Atlantic to England, from where, after a thorough refit, she had now returned.

Early in 1778 Sir Peter sailed south from Rhode Island to take command of the Jamaica station. As Mr Hargood was now considered one of Sir Peter's followers, he was also turned over to the *Bristol* and on the 13th February arrived in that ship at Port Royal. [The Port of Kingston on the south shore of Jamaica.]

Sir Peter Parker was much too zealous and prudent a man to allow his ship to lie rotting in harbour, to the injury as well as the health of the ship's company, and accordingly we find the *Bristol* to have been one of the keenest cruisers on the station.

For the early part of his time Sir Peter Parker constantly took charge of the convoys himself, and from the excellent order in which the ship was kept, the *Bristol* was able to become formidable to the fast-sailing privateers which infested the West Indies, and who watched every opportunity of picking up straggling ships.

On one occasion in May 1778 an American – or rebel privateer as they were at that time designated – succeeded in capturing one of the Admiral's convoy, a ship named the *St George*; but the British crew overpowered the American prize crew and rejoined the convoy. The privateer was seen on the next day, and the *Bristol* gave chase to her, but the brig managed to effect her escape under one of the keys.[1]

No one knew better than Admiral Parker how pirates got up to their tricks. A favourite one was to sail up to the intended victim flying the colours of its own country, or one with which it was politically aligned. Then, as the two ships came within gunshot, down came the Union Jack, or whatever flag the pirate was flying, and up went a red or, more commonly, a black flag, sometimes emblazoned with a skull and crossbones or similar macabre design.

The conflict between Britain and America had proved a godsend to the pirates in the Caribbean and the Atlantic. Some made enormous fortunes by seizing sugar and slaves. They divided the profits among them in a most democratic way, every man to his share. Normally they fled at sight of a warship, but some who were slow sailers, or who found themselves facing contrary winds, were caught and brought to justice and were either imprisoned or hanged.

During the whole of this year Mr Hargood continued to be thus employed; and the ship captured, in her various cruises, many valuable merchant ships and privateers.

The unfortunate obscurity in which this early portion of Mr

24

Hargood's life is involved deprives us doubtless of many interesting anecdotes of his 'hair-breadth scapes'. [However] it must have been about this time that he suffered a most perilous shipwreck, which he alone of the crew survived. The incident is one of the few of which he was in the habit of speaking; and from the fact that none of the ships he belonged to were wrecked, we must conclude the circumstance to have occurred at this period of his life, when he might have been absent from his ship in charge of a prize.

It was in the *Bristol* that Mr Hargood first made the acquaintance of Nelson and Collingwood; by both of whom he was ever afterwards held in the highest esteem.

These two young men, whom William Hargood now met for the first time, were destined to play an important part in his future life. Both were older than him, Nelson by four years, Collingwood by twelve. Totally opposite in appearance, they were also diverse in character, except in the virtues of courage and loyalty which both so obviously displayed.

Nelson, the parson's son from Norfolk, who had the temerity to go to sea against his uncle's advice, was below middle height. Now, wasted by some of the fevers to which men on the West Indian Station invariably succumbed, he looked sickly and frail, 'a mere boy of a captain' as someone who saw him a short time later exclaimed. Highly strung and emotional, he also possessed the most captivating charm.

Nelson was first brought to Admiral Parker's attention by his Captain, William Locker, an old friend of Parker's on whose recommendation Parker took him on board the *Bristol* as his third lieutenant. Captain Locker, on losing Nelson, appointed Collingwood in his place as first lieutenant of the frigate *Lowestoft*, which he commanded.

Cuthbert Collingwood, or 'Coll' as Nelson called him, came of sound Northumbrian stock. A handsome man, strong-featured in his portraits, he was of substantial build. Shy to the point of appearing aloof, he nonetheless possessed an exceptional ability to command. Renowned for forbidding the fearsome punishment of the 'cat' for all except the most heinous of crimes, he yet maintained a discipline on his ships which was the envy of most of his contemporaries. 'Send him to Collingwood' was Nelson's catch-phrase when, in his later years, any of his captains complained of a particularly disobedient man.

Hargood first served aboard the *Bristol* with Nelson for a brief three months.

On the 20th July 1778, Lieutenant Horatio Nelson joined the *Bristol*, from the *Lowestoft*, as third lieutenant, and continued third until September, from which time until the 20th December, he was first lieutenant. Lieutenant Collingwood succeeded Nelson (who had been appointed to command the *Badger*) as first of the *Bristol*, and remained in her until June 1779, when he also followed Nelson in command of the *Badger*. While Collingwood was first lieutenant, the *Bristol*, in heaving-down at Port Royal, sprung her mainmast. Mr James McNamara was a lieutenant of the *Bristol* at this time, as was also Lieutenant Timothy Kelly.

Promotion at length rewarded Mr Hargood's continuous and good service. On the 13th January, 1780, being then in his eighteenth year, he received his commission as lieutenant of the *Port Royal*, 14 gun sloop, the command of which ship had been conferred upon Lieutenant Timothy Kelly, with the rank of commander.

It is a very remarkable coincidence that Mr Hargood should have succeeded Lieutenant Manley Dixon [both] in this, his first commissioned appointment, and in the last commission he ever received, that of Commander-in-Chief at Plymouth, [when] he again followed the same officer, by then Admiral Sir Manley Dixon.

4

THE SIEGE OF PENSACOLA

1780, the year in which Lieutenant Hargood obtained his commission, is marked by the fearful ravages of one of those dreadful hurricanes which occasionally visit the West Indian Islands. The ships of the British Navy suffered terrible damage – some disappeared without trace - and there were many casualties.

The *Thunderer*, 74 guns, belonging to a squadron detached in charge of a convoy by Sir Peter Parker, was overtaken by the hurricane on the 5th October; at six o'clock of the evening of that day she was lost sight of by her squadron and was seen no more. The *Grafton*, bearing Rear-Admiral Rowley's flag, was completely dismasted, and she was every minute expected to go down. The four other ships – *Trident*, *Ruby*, *Bristol*, and *Hector* – suffered severely in the hurricane, and when the squadron, in a shattered state, returned to Port Royal harbour, scarcely a person on board had wholly escaped suffering from broken legs, and others from severe bruises and contusions. The *Stirling Castle* was lost on the Silver Keys; and the *Phoenix*, frigate, was wrecked on the island of Cuba. The West India Islands everywhere presented fearful marks of this devastating tempest.

This awful visitation reached St Lucia [one of the Windward Islands, which lies north-east of Barbados and south of Martinique] on the 10th October. All the barracks and huts on the island were blown down, and the ships in the roadstead driven out to sea. The *Amazon*, frigate, Captain the Hon William Clement Finch, miraculously escaped foundering, but with the loss of all her masts, and about twenty men drowned.

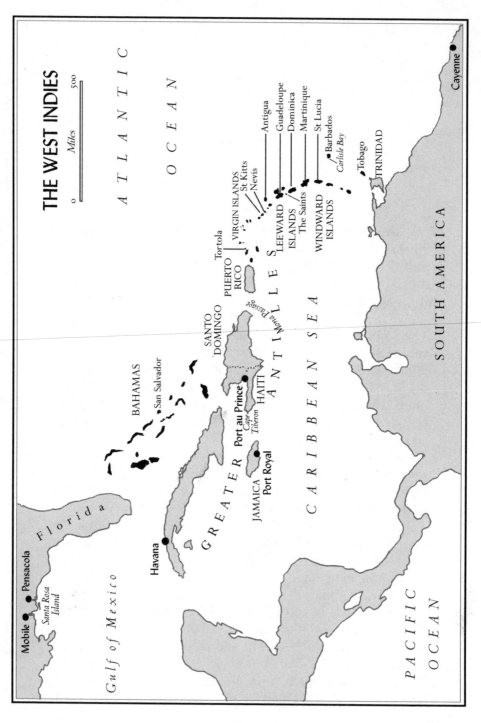

THE WEST INDIES

Miles

0   500

ATLANTIC

OCEAN

Mobile
Pensacola
Santa Rosa Island

Gulf of Mexico

Florida

Havana

BAHAMAS
San Salvador

GREATER

JAMAICA
Port Royal

Port au Prince
Cape Tiberon
HAITI

SANTO DOMINGO

Mona Passage

PUERTO RICO

Tortola
VIRGIN ISLANDS

ANTILLES

Antigua
Guadeloupe
Dominica
Martinique
St Lucia

St Kitts
Nevis

LEEWARD ISLANDS

The Saints

WINDWARD ISLANDS

Barbados
Carlisle Bay

Tobago
TRINIDAD

CARIBBEAN SEA

PACIFIC OCEAN

SOUTH AMERICA

Cayenne

28

The *Vengeance*, 74, sustained great injury, and in the harbour of St Lucia, the *Beaver's* prize was wrecked, with the loss of many of her crew. The *Ajax* and the *Montague*, 74-gun ships, were driven out to sea where they sustained much damage; and the *Egmont*, 74, also driven out of St. Lucia, was dismasted and obliged to run for Jamaica. The *Blonde*, 32, and the *Camelion*, 14, foundered with all their crews; and the *Andromeda* and *Laurel*, 28-gun frigates, were driven on shore at Martinique, and only a few of their crews saved. Every ship on the station received more or less damage.

The *Port Royal*, amongst all these disasters, escaped uninjured, having been dispatched, with the 20-gun ship *Mentor* (Captain Robert Deans) in the month of April to Pensacola [in West Florida] in order to co-operate with the land forces in the Royal defence of that place and there the *Port Royal* remained throughout the year.

During the 17th century the French and Spanish vied with each other for possession of the southern part of North America. The town of Pensacola had been founded by the Spanish to counter French claims. Now in the hands of the British, it had become an important trading centre for both exports and imports around the world.

Against the British settlements in West Florida a powerful Spanish force, under Don Bernard de Galvez, was assembling. Mobile was attacked and capitulated on 14 March 1780. Then Pensacola became the next target.

Mobile, at the head of the bay of that name, is only about 35 miles due west of Pensacola as the crow flies. Pensacola is situated on the western side of the entrance to a deeply indented bay in the Gulf of Mexico. The shore is low and sandy, but the town, on a slight acclivity, is built in a parallelogram form which in those days extended to about a mile.

Don Bernard de Galvez, the governor of the Spanish colony of Louisiana, and an officer of great ability, deeming the garrison of Pensacola much stronger than it really was, occupied much time in making his preparations for the attack.

The command of the British forces at Pensacola was vested in Major-General John Campbell, and consisted of detachments from the 16th and 60th regiments of infantry, the

German regiment (Waldeck's) together with Maryland and Pennsylvanian loyalists, two provincial corps, and a small detachment of the royal artillery. To these were added some of the inhabitants, Negroes and others, who dreaded the return of Spanish power among them.

Major-General Campbell, having received information of the intention of De Galvez to attack the place, exerted himself to the uttermost in strengthening the fortifications and adding new works to Fort George. The naval force consisted only of the *Mentor* and *Port Royal*, and the whole garrison amounted to no more than twelve hundred men.

Don Galvez, having at length collected a force of twelve sail of the line, and a large body of transports, sailed from the Havannah [the port on the north-west of Cuba, on the Gulf of Mexico] for Pensacola on the 23rd February 1781. On the following day this fleet was further increased by the junction of four French sail of the line under the Chevalier Monteil. [However] a heavy gale of wind on the following day [the 25th] overtook and dispersed the fleets, which were obliged to return to Havannah greatly damaged.

Don Galvez, however, with a division of five ships of the line and some frigates, which were uninjured, together with transports containing five hundred cavalry and five thousand foot, put to sea on the 1st of March, and on the 9th arrived off the harbour of Pensacola.

In the night the Spaniards effected a landing on the island of Santa Rosa, and on the following day the squadron made an attempt to force their passage into the harbour. But with such warmth were they received by the forts, and the guns of the two ships, that the squadron was repulsed with much loss.

The strength opposed to the garrison, however, was such as could not be successfully resisted for any length of time.

[The Spanish had gained possession of a small fort on Santa Rosa, the island that commanded the entrance to the harbour, and could afford to wait.] On the 19th March they made a second attempt in which they succeeded. [Nonetheless] Fort George and the sloops of war still kept the shipping at bay, and until the middle of April the progress of the besiegers was very slow. But Don Josef Solano, with the French and Spanish ships, and a reinforcement of troops from Mobile, having arrived, the defence of Pensacola became desperate.

In this emergency the service rendered by the crew of the two ships was gratefully acknowledged by the governor, General Chester. Lieutenant Hargood, in command of a party consisting of two midshipmen and fifty men from the *Port Royal*, was employed on shore at the Royal Navy Redoubt and at the advanced batteries during the whole of this harassing siege, in which he lost one midshipman – Mr John Blein – and twelve seamen killed.

The contest would have been maintained for a much longer period had it not been for an accident that threw the garrison into the greatest distress.

On the morning of the 8th of May, a shell, thrown by the besiegers, fell near the door of the magazine of the advanced redoubt, in which, it is believed, Lieutenant Hargood was serving at the time. Exploding, it burst it open and communicated with the powder in the magazine.

The effect of the explosion was terrific: the redoubt was reduced to a heap of rubbish; forty-eight soldiers, twenty-seven seamen and one Negro were killed and twenty-four men dangerously wounded.

By this time only two flank works remained, but these were so vigorously defended by Captain Johnstone, the officer in command, that the enemy were repulsed in their first advance upon the ruined battery, and time afforded to carry out the wounded.

Governor Chester and General Campbell, finding themselves so hardly pushed, and almost all the shot and ammunition exhausted, at length came to the conclusion that their defence could only, at the most, be protracted for a few days, at a great expense of life. [Therefore] they ordered a flag of truce to be displayed on the afternoon of the same day on which the accident occurred to the redoubt.

The terms granted by Don Bernard de Galvez were highly honourable to the defenders; and thus, after sixty-one days from the landing upon Santa Rosa, and twelve from the opening of the trenches, the Spaniards regained possession of Pensacola and the remaining parts of West Florida.

The loss to the British in this siege was ninety-five men killed and about fifty wounded, principally by the explosion of the magazine. The *Mentor* was burnt during the siege, but the *Port Royal* was delivered up to the Spaniards, agreeably to the terms of the capitulation; and the garrison were suffered to depart in a polacre for the Havannah and New York on the 4th July.

William Hargood's feelings as he saw the *Port Royal*, his first command and his pride and joy, being surrendered can be well be imagined. Nevertheless it may have been some consolation that at last he was being sent home.

From New York he sailed back to England, having been away for six years. He had left at the age of fourteen and now came back a young man approaching twenty. His family found that the little boy who had left them, pale-faced from the English climate, had returned still small in stature, but strong and muscular in person and bronzed by the wind and sun. What tales he had to tell them of all that he had seen and done. How proud they were of his achievements. They must have made him the talk of the parish where many sought to shake his hand.

Several of the young ladies doubtless donned their prettiest bonnets in the hope of catching his eye. Despite his lack of inches he cut a striking figure in his lieutenant's uniform. The coat of rather bright blue had white cuffs and lapels, gold anchor-buttons and long tails. His cloth waistcoat, knee breeches and stockings were white. Most striking of all was his three-cornered black hat, generally worn 'athwartships', and embellished with a cockade. His naval sword, when he wore it, was slung in a belt worn over the shoulder.

We do not know if he made any romantic attachments. If he did they were of short duration. On the pay of a junior lieutenant (under a hundred pounds per annum) and with little or no money of his own, he could barely afford to marry until he achieved a higher rank. He may have left broken hearts behind him, but his mind was set on his career. Most naval officers without prospects, other than advancement in the service, dreaded a long time ashore. The Lords of the Admiralty, however, had noted Hargood's efficiency. They summoned him after five months.

Lieutenant Hargood did not remain long enough unemployed to suffer his abilities to go to decay or his sword to rust. In the month of December, in the same year [1781] he was appointed fourth lieutenant of the *Magnificent*, of 74 guns, fitting for sea in Portsmouth harbour, under the command of Captain Robert Linzee. Two months later she was ready to put to sea.

5

THE BATTLE OF THE SAINTS

The *Magnificent*, true to her name, was a sight lovely to behold. 'A ship of the line under full sail must have been one of the most beautiful of the works of man.'[1]

Carrying seventy guns, she was a third-rate ship-of-the line. It had taken 3,000 loads of oak (approximately 2,000 trees) and 400 loads of elm for planks below the waterline to build her. Known as a 'two-decker', because she had two main decks, she actually had top decks as well.

From the Captain's cabin, below the poop in the stern, a few steps led down to the quarterdeck which continued as far as the break, just above the mainmast. From here gangways, on either side of the waist of the ship, ran forward to the forecastle, where hung the ship's bell. Here on both sides were ranged the new guns, introduced only three years previously in 1779, called 'carronades'. The invention of one Mr Gascoign, they were named after the town in Scotland where they were first cast. Small and squat, only two to five feet long, they nonetheless spat out balls of up to twelve pounds in weight. Deadly in a close action, they caused such fearful damage to the hull of a ship that they were dubbed 'smashers' or 'devil guns'. Soon the French would experience their catastrophic effect. Through the deck of the forecastle came the chimney of the galley that brought some warmth to the sick bays which adjoined. Further still on the 'beakhead' were the 'heads', the primitive lavatories which were simply holes above the sea.

Below, on the main deck the 18-pounder guns were ranged on either side, while on the next level, known as the lower deck, the mighty 32-pounders were mounted correspondingly along the full length of the ship.

This (as already related in Chapter 1) was where most of the crew slept and ate. Aft on this deck was the lieutenant's wardroom, while forward was the galley. Here also, by the hawse holes through which the anchor cables passed, was the 'manger' in which livestock were penned. Lower still, below the water-line, was the orlop deck, which contained the midshipmen's berth, the cockpit and the spirit room. Finally, at the very bottom of the ship was the hold, considered the safest place for the magazine, and where every kind of equipment such as spare sails, spars and ropes, together with the water casks and provisions, were stored.

On the 7th February, 1782, the *Magnificent* sailed from Spithead, for the purpose of joining the fleet in the West Indies, a division of which had sailed only a few days before. On the next day she fell in with the *Valiant*, Captain Samuel Goodall, and shortly afterwards with the *Agamemnon*, Captain Caldwell, and these ships made sail in company.

The *Magnificent* reached Carlisle Bay, Barbadoes, on the 20th March, from whence she departed for Gros Islet Bay, St Lucia, at which place she joined Rear-Admiral Sir Samuel Hood, with ten sail of the line and two frigates, lying at anchor in the bay.

Rear-Admiral Rodney, re-appointed to the command, had in fact sailed into Barbados a month and a day before them (on the 19 February) with twelve ships of the line. Among them was the *Namur*, her captain Robert Fanshawe and her fourth lieutenant James Nicoll Morris, son of the captain who, when in command of the *Bristol*, had died of his wounds after the battle off Charleston.

Arriving at St Lucia, Rodney had found Admiral Hood, who, in the previous December had returned from the American coast, to take temporary command. Hood did have twenty-two ships of the line but most were so battered as to be barely seaworthy. Faced with a French force of thirty battleships in much better repair, he had been unable to prevent the loss of St Kitts. Nonetheless, during the action to defend the island, he had shown the competence which made Nelson afterwards laud him as 'the greatest sea officer I ever knew ... equally great in all situations which an admiral can be placed in'.

Hood, now aged fifty-eight, was, like Nelson, the son of a country parson. He had, however, not gone to sea until he was sixteen and thus had received a better education than most of his contemporaries in the navy. An intellectual, an expert in astronomy, geography and shipbuilding, he was also a philanthropist with a real understanding of men who genuinely loved him in return.[2] In defiance of the hierarchy of the Navy he had begun to take his captains and junior officers into his confidence to explain to them what he intended to do, a tactic which Nelson emulated with such conspicuous success.

In this instance, Hood, with his officers' co-operation, brilliantly outmanoeuvred the French Admiral de Grasse, by enticing him from his safe anchorage in Frigate Bay at St Kitts, and then, once de Grasse was safely out to sea, seizing the anchorage himself.

On news of Rodney's arrival, Hood had then again outwitted de Grasse by taking the fleet to sea under cover of darkness. Under the very noses of the French he got clear away to join his chief, whom he found, on 25 February, off Antigua. Following their rendezvous the two British fleets, now of much the same strength, had retired to their respective bases, Fort Royal and Gros Islet Bay, St Lucia.

The plan of Admiral de Grasse was to join up with the Spanish squadron lying at Havana and attack Jamaica. However, following the usual French strategy, he hoped to get away with this without having to fight the British fleet. From Gros Islet Bay Rodney watched and waited, determined to make him fight. At last on the evening of 7 April came word that the French fleet was under way.

The *Magnificent*, with the *Agamemnon*, was ordered to reconnoitre the French fleet, then lying, ready for sea, in Fort Royal Bay, Martinique. This she accordingly did, and on the 2nd April counted thirty-five sail at anchor there. With this intelligence the *Magnificent* returned to Gros Islet Bay, where Sir George Rodney was waiting with thirty-six sail of the line, ready to put to sea, at a moment's warning, to meet the enemy.

The *Magnificent* and the *Agamemnon* continued to watch the enemy's movements, and on the morning of the 8th April, observed the French ships, consisting of thirty sail of the line and a number of transports, to be getting under way. This news was quickly conveyed to Sir George Rodney; and standing over for St Lucia, at noon the *Magnificent* was joined by her fleet. The remainder of the day was employed in chasing the enemy, who, being to windward, did not appear inclined to come to an action. On the night of the 8th the British fleet brought to on the starboard tack, and at daybreak on the 9th the French fleet was observed close under the west end of Martinique.

The *Magnificent*, on this eventful morning, to which in some measure may be attributed the subsequent brilliant victory of the 12th [Battle of The Saints], belonged to Rear-Admiral Hood's division, which formed the van of the British fleet. This division having a breeze of wind, while the centre and rear divisions were becalmed, was enabled to bring the enemy's fleet to action; and Count de Grasse, the French Admiral, whose policy it was to avoid, if possible, an action, was tempted by the isolated position of this portion of the British fleet, to commence the action, deeming himself tolerably sure of obtaining a victory.

But the more immediate cause of the French Admiral's bringing on the action was that, from the variableness of the wind, the French fleet was somewhat dispersed, and one ship being becalmed, and at a distance to leeward, he was induced to bear up to her support. [This was the 74-gun *Zélé* which had twice collided with two other ships.] At ten o'clock in the morning the ship in which Lieutenant Hargood was serving opened her fire upon the French line, and she continued firing for half-an-hour, but at too great a distance to do much execution, or receive any great injury, if we except several shot between wind and water.

As the breeze became more general, the British Admiral was enabled to join his van division, and the French fleet then hauled to the wind and made sail, having received by far the worst of the action. At two o'clock in the afternoon the enemy tacked and stood to the southward, and the signal for battle was hauled down.

The situation of the British van, when thus exposed to the attack of the whole French fleet, was very critical, and nothing but the firmness and good seamanship of Sir Samuel Hood could have sufficed to save the division entire. Eight British ships – the *Magnificent* being one – were engaged with fifteen French ships for a considerable time, without the possibility of receiving any help from their own fleet.

The remaining part of the 9th and all of the 10th of April was occupied in chasing the French fleet, but without any visible advantage. Accidents to two of the French fleet, however, which had suffered in the action of the 9th, favoured the British, for, at daybreak on the morning of the 11th, it was observed that the two line-of-battle ships were disabled, and a long way to leeward of their fleet. Sir George Rodney immediately made the signal for a general chase, and the pursuit lasted throughout the day.

The *Magnificent*, not being the slowest sailer, had gained considerably upon the two French ships, and as it was at that time blowing a strong breeze of wind the chase became very interesting; but, with much gallantry, Compte de Grasse refused to allow those ships to fall into the hands of their pursuers, and finding it impossible to save them otherwise than with his whole fleet, he bore up at four o'clock in the afternoon to their support. Sir George Rodney then called in the chasing ships, which were far advanced, and formed the order of sailing in line to receive the enemy's attack. The *Magnificent* accordingly bore up to rejoin her fleet; but the French Admiral, having effected his object, again hauled to the wind.

The next morning – being the far-famed 12th of April – the French fleet was discovered bearing west, and to the leeward of the British. At seven o'clock in the morning the Admiral made the signal for the leading British ships – one of which was the *Magnificent* – to try to cut off a part of the enemy's fleet running alongshore for Guadeloupe; but the manoeuvres of the French fleet being directed to support them, the chasing ships were recalled, and the whole formed in a line to meet the enemy. At a little before eight o'clock the Admiral made the signal for battle, and at eight for a closer engagement.

They were now lying south of Guadeloupe, close to the three small islands, collectively known as The Saints, from which the battle takes its name.

The *Magnificent*, now with her division in the rear, opened her fire at half past eight. She received in return the fire of the whole French line passing on the opposite tack. By ten o'clock the wind had died away and the *Magnificent* ceased firing, as the ship was so enshrouded in her own smoke that it was impossible for the men to distinguish friends from foes.

The density of the smoke was caused by a sudden lull in the wind. Then suddenly a breeze sprang up which forced the close-hauled French ships aback, while allowing the British ships to luff. Gaps appeared in the French line and Rodney saw his chance. In his flaghip *Formidable*, he led six ships through the line. Immediately behind him was the *Namur* with young Lieutenant Morris aboard, surrounded by cheering men. Ahead of the *Formidable,* the massive 90-gun three-decker *Duke* held her course so that the enemy ships between them, with their sails aback, were bombarded from either side. Broadside after broadside thundered into their hulls. Now the destructive power of the carronades was brought home in full effect. They did such tremendous execution that some of the French crews, completely demoralized, surrendered almost before firing a shot.[3]

> When, as the wind strengthened, the smoke at length cleared away, the *Magnificent* was found to be close to the French Admiral and a few ships of the division, and entirely separated from her own fleet. She accordingly recommenced firing, and until noon engaged the *Ville de Paris* and two other ships. Captain Linzee then seeing the *Warrior* to be hard pressed, wore to her support, and in doing so exposed his ship to a raking fire from the ships he had been engaging; but the French ships, firing high, did no great damage to her except for her masts and sails. On closing the *Warrior*, the two ships bore up to rejoin their division, engaging such ships of the enemy as they passed.

By this time most of the defeated had fled, ignoring de Grasse's frantic signals for them to reform. His flagship, the *Ville de Paris*, however, was too badly damaged to escape. By evening she had surrendered to Hood's flagship *Barfleur* and the French Admiral himself was a prisoner on Rodney's ship *Formidable*. Hood was furious with Rodney for missing the chance of taking more prizes by continuing the pursuit of the defeated French ships. 'Relations between them became strained to the point of breaking.' However, despite this disagreement with his superior officer, Hood himself was recognized as the hero of the hour. His grateful monarch, George III, lauding him as 'the most brilliant Officer of this war'.

> After this time it does not appear that the *Magnificent* was again in a position to effect any further service. Considering the part borne by this ship her loss was very trifling, amounting only to six seamen killed and twelve wounded; [however] her

lower masts were so much cut that it was found necessary to fish them [to put a sleeve on, probably of cast iron, to hold the mast firmly in place] and her sails, and standing [the stays and shrouds] and running rigging [wires and ropes] had received much injury.

This well-fought battle – which earned for the gallant Rodney a peerage[4] – terminated, as is well known, in the capture of the following ships –*Ville de Paris*, 110 [guns], 74 gun-ships, *Glorieux*, *Câesar*, and *Hector*; and 64 gun-ship *Ardent*. The *Diademe*, French 74, was sunk in the action. The French fleet were then suffered to escape, or rather did escape by their superior sailing. Sir George Rodney proceeded to Jamaica with the body of the fleet and the prizes; but thinking it possible that there still might be found some of the disabled French ships in the neighbourhood of the islands, he dispatched Sir Samuel Hood in the *Barfleur*, with the *Magnificent*, *Monarch*, *Valiant*, and *Belliqueux*, to look after them.

On the 19th, being the day after the squadron left the Admiral, being then in the Mona Passage, a strange sail was descried at daylight in the south-west quarter, and soon afterwards four sails more; upon which Sir Samuel Hood made the signal for a general chase. The strangers were soon discovered to be French, and of force; and at a little past noon the signal was made to engage.

At about two o'clock the *Magnificent* was directed, by signal, to alter her course three points, and to chase one of the strangers which had separated from her consorts. She accordingly did so, and at about twenty minutes past two opened her fire upon the chase, which was returned with much gallantry; but after a running fight of about forty minutes the chase surrendered, and proved to be *L'Aimable*, a French 40-gun frigate.

In this engagement the *Magnificent* had four men killed and eight wounded. Of the remaining [French] ships three were captured: viz. the *Caton* and *Jason* of 64 guns each, and the *Ceres*, 18. The *Astrea*, frigate, which was the fifth, escaped. The squadron continued to cruise off Cuba for some short time, after which it proceeded to Port Royal, Jamaica, arriving there on the 26th May [1782].

The *Magnificent* soon after this was in a very perilous situation: being in company with the *Monarch*, 74, on the 23rd of July, she got aground on the shoals of Savannah la Mar [Jamaica]. After much hard labour, however, she was 'hove off', but was so leaky as to render it necessary to keep the chain pumps constantly going; and the ship proceeded with her squadron to Halifax, where she arrived on the 23rd September. At this place the ship was hove down and found to have received considerable injury.

After having undergone the necessary repairs at Halifax, she departed on the 1st December, and on the 9th encountered a heavy gale of wind, which blew the close-reefed main topsail out of the boltrope. A worse misfortune followed; for, from the heavy head sea, she pitched away her mizenmast, which, falling forward, carried away the maintopsail yard in the slings, and killed five men besides seriously injuring several others.

The *Magnificent* proceeded to Carlisle Bay, where she anchored on the 30th December, and from thence departed to Gros Islet Bay, St Lucia.

Here, on the 19th January 1783, another accident occurred by which three men were badly wounded. The ships in the bay, in honour of the Queen's birthday, were firing, as usual, a royal salute, in the course of which a shot from the *St Eustatia*, which most carelessly, had not been drawn, entered the *Magnificent* and wounded three of her crew.

On the 12th February the *Magnificent* sailed from Gros Islet Bay for a cruise. With her went the 64 gun-ships *Prudent* and *St Albans* [Captains Adam Barclay and Charles Inglis.] On the 16th the sight of a strange sail sent the *Magnificent* off in pursuit. By six o'clock she had neared sufficiently to make out the chase to be a frigate. At eight o'clock, it being then dark, the frigate began firing her chase guns, but the *Magnificent*, at a quarter-past nine, succeeded in getting alongside, and in fifteen minutes compelled her to strike, and took possession of her. The frigate proved to be *La Concorde*, of 36 guns and 300 men, commanded by M. le Chevalier du Clesmaur.

After the ship was captured, her maintopsail caught fire and it was considered necessary to cut away the mainmast to extinguish it. The *Prudent* and *St Albans* did not arrive up until two hours afterwards. The *Magnificent* took the prize in tow, and conveyed her to St John's, Antigua.

This was the last service performed in the *Magnificent* for the war soon came to an end. [In September 1783, a peace treaty signed in Paris brought the War of American Independence to a close.] Seven months later, on 21 April, she sailed for England in company with nine sail of the line. The voyage took seven weeks and she arrived at Spithead on 11 June. She was paid off in Portsmouth harbour on the 27th.

6

PIRATES, THE PRINCE, A SCANDAL AND NELSON'S WEDDING.

Lieutenant William Hargood, having been paid off from the *Magnificent* was not long unemployed. The monotony of shore life was tedious, not to mention expensive, and he jumped at the chance of being third officer of the *Hebe*, commanded by Captain (later Admiral Sir Edward) Thornborough. The Captain was renowned for having a very short fuse.

The jealousy of this officer for the honour of the British flag was shown only two days before prior to Lieutenant Hargood's joining the *Hebe*. Being on a cruise in the Channel, the *Hebe* fell in with a Dutch frigate, the captain of which, not paying the required homage of lowering his topgallant sails to the English colours, Captain Thornborough fired a shot at her to remind the Dutch of the custom. The demand was instantly complied with, and, in addition, the frigate fired a salute of nine guns.

Lieutenant Hargood joined the *Hebe* in Plymouth Sound, and here his knowledge of seamanship must have been brought into use, for the ship, being stationed in the channel, was constantly cruising for the suppression of smuggling, then carried on to a considerable extent. While thus employed she gave chase, on the 18th June [1784] to a large French lugger, and a most tedious chase it was; but at length the lugger gave signs of having surrendered, and lowered her sails immediately under the *Hebe*'s bows. Before, however the *Hebe* could shorten sail, or possession could be taken of the nimble Frenchman, the *Hebe* had shot ahead of her, and the lugger being then on the weather quarter of the frigate, rehoisted her sails and made her escape. This trying service continued until the following spring.

In the month of June, 1785, the *Hebe* was honoured by receiving on board as third lieutenant (Lieutenant Hargood having become second) his Royal Highness Prince William Henry. At the same time Commodore Leveson Gower hoisted his broad pendant in the *Hebe* and proceeded on a voyage round Scotland and Ireland.

On the 16th September Commodore Gower left the *Hebe* and she then continued her old round of Channel cruising with his Royal Highness on board.

Prince William began to throw his weight about once the Commodore had gone. Bored by the monotony of sailing up and down the same stretch of sea, he became truculent. While subservient to the Captain's authority, he considered the other officers to be barely worthy of respect. Accustomed as he was to the adulation of courtiers, he did not take kindly to being treated without the deference he had come to expect as his right. The little second lieutenant in particular, upon whom, in a literal sense, he could look down his nose, would, he felt sure, be only too keen to ingratiate himself with his monarch's son. Certainly a man of such inferior social standing would not dare to stand in his way.

He was soon to be disillusioned. Hargood was no man's pawn.

The *Hebe* was at anchor at some port [what port is not clearly defined, but most probably either Plymouth of Portsmouth]. Captain Thornborough and the first lieutenant being on shore, Lieutenant Hargood became commanding officer. A signal was made by the flagship for a lieutenant from the *Hebe*, and Lieutenant Hargood ordered his Royal Highness, as the junior lieutenant, to repair on board and answer it.

The Prince demurred, as it was probable he had not often been sent on such a service, but Lieutenant Hargood remained firm, and was prepared to proceed to the utmost extremities to enforce obedience to the rules of the navy. [In an officer's case this meant court martial: only ordinary seamen were flogged. However, fortunately it proved unnecessary to go to such extremes!]

His Royal Highness, who, upon consideration, found he was in the wrong, obeyed the orders of his senior officer; and so far from entertaining any feeling of unkindness in consequence, it is believed that this transaction, marking as it did, Lieutenant Hargood's paramount respect for the formalities of the profession to which both belonged, was the commencement of that honourable friendship which ever afterwards existed between them.

One can imagine the predicament in which Hargood found himself placed. Convinced of the justness of his action, he must nonetheless have had visions of swinging from the yardarm for his temerity in confronting a prince of the royal blood. Nonetheless Prince William, despite the circumstances of his birth, was a simple man at heart. He also appears to have recognized and respected the sterling character of the little lieutenant who had had the courage to stand up to him and put him so firmly in his place.

Hargood, for his part, must have been well aware of the loss of face which the Prince had suffered in owning up to being wrong. Perhaps the two shook hands in a gentlemanly way. At any rate some form of reconciliation took place. Each then came to realize the qualities of the other to the point that, from this inauspicious beginning, a friendship developed between them which, on the evidence of both of them, lasted for the rest of their lives.

In the spring of 1786 Prince William, having completed his full period of service to qualify him for promotion, was removed into the 28-gun frigate *Pegasus* as first lieutenant. He received his commission as post captain on the 14th April. He had not forgotten his old messmate Lieutenant Hargood, whom he chose to go with him as second, subsequent to his becoming first lieutenant. The first lieutenant of the *Pegasus*, from the time his Royal Highness became captain until the 20th June, 1787, was Lieutenant Isaac Schomberg, well known as a compiler of the Naval Chronology.

Joseph Allen does not describe the traumas that then took place on board the *Pegasus*. Obviously he did not want to displease Maria Hargood, the Admiral's widow, who had commissioned him to write the book, and in particular he knew that must not offend Queen Adelaide, King William's widow, to whom Maria Hargood was to dedicate his work.

In fact a situation had arisen which, within the confines of a battleship, must have been both awkward and extremely unpleasant, particularly for the officers on board. The confrontation arose from Rear-Admiral Hood's choice of Isaac Schomberg to serve as first lieutenant on the *Pegasus* under the Prince. Hood knew Schomberg, who had been first lieutenant of HMS *Canada* during the action off St Kitts, and thought him a reliable man. Thus he recommended him when King George III asked him to find a mentor for Prince William during his first command.

Unfortunately the two disliked each other from the start. Schomberg, at the age of thirty-three, resented taking orders from a younger man. The Prince was determined to assert his authority. And so the trouble began. The two disagreed frequently and were already at loggerheads almost as the *Pegasus* put to sea.

The *Pegasus* passed the first few months in a visit to the Channel Islands, but on the 6th June left Plymouth for North America and the West Indies. On her voyage out she met a heavy gale from the southward, in which she was found to labour very heavily and to leak much. On the 14th June the *Rose* joined company, and both ships sailed together until they were separated by a fog. The *Pegasus* anchored in Trespassey Harbour, Newfoundland, on the 27th June, and remained there and at Placentia Harbour till September.

From Placentia the *Pegasus* departed for the West India islands, and at Dominica fell in with the *Boreas*, 28, commanded by Captain Nelson. It was at this period that the friendship, which existed between his Royal Highness and Nelson, commenced.

Again Allen avoids making any mention of the drama connected with this friendship which was now taking place on board the *Pegasus*. The friction between Prince William and Schomburg finally reached a climax when Schomberg took a boat ashore without permission. The Prince, losing his temper, wrote a reprimand accusing him of neglect of duty, whereupon Schomberg demanded a court martial to clear his name.

This was a dispute which could, if handled tactfully, have been settled without further delay. Alas, it was not. Captain Horatio Nelson, as the senior officer on the station, received Schomberg's request. Already a friend of the Prince, and keen to ingratiate himself further to the advancement of his career, he agreed to comply with it. This, however, meant waiting until enough post captains could be gathered to form a court. Meanwhile Schomberg, to his fury, was held under arrest.

The affair dragged on for months until at last a mediator, in the form of Commodore Alan Gardner, appeared to save the day. Having managed to convince the Prince that he did not have enough evidence for a conviction he then persuaded Schomberg to withdraw his demand for a court martial. The whole unsavoury and much publicized incident thus appeared to have come to an end. Nonetheless, it did have a repercussion as far as Nelson was concerned. Hood, in a recently discovered letter to Nelson, dated 1790, told him quite plainly that his mishandling of the Schomberg affair was the main reason for his being kept without a ship, on half pay, from 1787- 93. Meanwhile Joseph Allen does give a brief description of a far happier event.

> At the marriage of Captain Nelson to Mrs Nesbit [on the island of Nevis] his Royal Highness gave away the bride and joined in the festivities incident upon that, by far, the happiest portion of the hero's life. Nelson's old shipmate, Lieutenant Hargood, was also a welcome guest.[1]

Nelson had first met Fanny as he always called her, when he had sailed into Nevis two years earlier in command of HMS *Boreas*. Born Frances Woolward, her father was the senior judge and her uncle President of the Council of the rich, sugar-growing, island upon which she had lived as a child. She had married a doctor, Josiah Nesbit, by whom she had had a son. With her husband she had moved to England where he had died, reportedly insane. Returning to Nevis, she had become her uncle's hostess and this was how Nelson found her, a still young and extremely attractive woman, in 1785.

They were married in Montpelier, the house on Fanny's uncle John Herbert's plantation, on 11 March 1787. Montpelier has vanished. Only the gateposts at the foot of the drive remain. Today one can but imagine the scene of the wedding which took place over two hundred years ago.

The colours of the sea and the coconut palms spring to mind. Below them the guests are gathered, the young officers, elegant in their uniforms, the women in their high-waisted muslin dresses, seeking shade from the burning sun. Somehow one hears the laughter, born on the wind from the sea, and the voices toasting the young captain and his bride, who together would soon sail away in the man- of-war lying in the bay.

Nelson and Fanny soon returned to England, as did Prince William and William Hargood, now first lieutenant of the *Pegasus*. Schomberg, in the meantime, had become first lieutenant on Hood's flagship, the *Barfleur*, proof that the Admiral considered him to have been unjustly treated in his contretemps with the Prince.

In the fall of the year, 1787, the *Pegasus* sailed for England, and after touching at Cork, arrived at Plymouth in January, 1788. In March his Royal Highness, with Lieutenant Hargood as his first lieutenant, and ship's company, were turned over to the 32-gun frigate *Andromeda,* and again departed for America and the West Indies.

Early one morning the *Andromeda* was nearly lost in a squall, owing to the infirmity of speech in the officer of the watch – Mr Jemmet Mainwaring, which rendered him incapable of giving orders to shorten sail. The ship was thrown on her beam ends. Lieutenant Hargood was at the time dressing, and the ladders having been unshipped while the decks were washed, he was pushed up the gunroom skylight on the shoulders of his messmates, and reaching the quarterdeck half-dressed, gave the necessary orders for taking the sail off the ship.

There are some advantages in being small. Certainly, on this occasion, had Hargood not been able to get through the skylight in his underclothes all on board the *Andromeda* would have been lost. The ship returned to England in the month of April 1789 and was paid off.

This was now a time of peace and many Naval officers found themselves redundant. However, this was not the case with Hargood who had made his mark with those in power in the Admiralty and with his friend the King's son.

48

In the month of June this year, the merits of Lieutenant Hargood were at length rewarded by promotion to the rank of master and commander, and in December of the same year he was appointed to command the *Swallow* sloop.

7

CAPTURE, REVOLUTION AND
COURT MARTIAL

During the time Captain Hargood commanded the *Swallow* he was employed principally on the Irish station . . . He had held this command not quite a twelvemonth when he received his post rank, and was superseded, on the 22nd November, 1790 by Captain Bissett. As it was a period of profound peace, Captain Hargood did not get another commission until the spring of 1792 when he was appointed to the command of the 24-gun ship *Hyaena*, which he joined in Hamoaze on the 25th April.

It was during this interval that, being unemployed, he was frequently in the company of his Royal Highness the Duke of Clarence [as Prince William was now known]. One day it happened that his Royal Highness and Captain Hargood were together on the Thames, in a small wherry boat rowed by one of the watermen, when the Duke, full of life, stood up in the boat, and began to move about in such a manner as to create much concern for the safety of the whole in the minds of both Captain Hargood and the waterman.

The circumstances being urgent, Captain Hargood resorted to some little coercion, and by this and persuasion at length induced the lively prince to sit down and remain quiet.

On quitting the boat, the waterman, not being at all aware of the quality of his passengers, spoke to his Royal Highness and told him that he probably owed his life to his companion; and when the unusual reward of a guinea for his fare at once imposed upon him silence and surprise.

Prince Willaim, by now subdued and probably sober, was plainly terrified that the news of his escapade would reach the ears of his father and cause a national scandal. William Hargood thereafter probably dismissed the incident from his mind, but Prince William, who had the wonderful memory of most of his family, certainly did not forget.

When his Royal Highness became king, His Majesty, only a few days afterwards, sent for his old shipmate, and recalled the incident to his remembrance, adding, 'You little thought at that time that you were saving the life of your future sovereign.'!

On the 4th May 1792 the *Hyaena* sailed from Plymouth for Madiera and the West Indies [the lieutenants were Farmary, Pridham, Epworth and Thomas Shirley]. She arrived at Madeira after a passage of only seven days, making in one day a run of two hundred and eighty-six miles, being upon the average twelve miles an hour. On the 15th May she sailed from Funchal, and arrived at Barbadoes on the 31st. Captain Hargood appears to have been actively employed on the station, and for some time was in the River Orinoka, from which he returned to Kingston, Jamaica.

Vessels of the description of the *Hyaena*, are, happily for the navy, now unknown in the service; and their successors, the small 28-gun frigates, are also rapidly disappearing. The 24-gun ships had a spar deck, and although latterly mounted with 32-pounder carronades, which added much to their efficiency, the *Hyaena* was armed with long guns, nine and six pounders only. The extra top weight of the quarterdeck and forecastle greatly impeded their sailing, while being frigate-built much more was expected of them.

It was this description of the ship which Captain Hargood commanded [written in 1841] and the sequel of her capture cannot now cause surprise if ever it did.

The *Hyaena* proved in all respects to be an unlucky ship for Hargood. He was laid low with an illness when aboard her, probably yellow fever then so virulent in the West Indies. Thought to be dead, he was just about to be stitched into a shroud to be thrown overboard when some sign of life was seen and the funeral abandoned.

Amongst the earliest events of the French revolutionary war of 1793, the capture of the *Hyaena* was numbered . . . The circumstances of the capture are fully detailed in the following letter of Captain Hargood to the senior officer on the Jamaica station, which, from its never having appeared in print, will be read with interest.

Port Royal, Jamaica,
June 28, 1793.

Sir'

I arrived here with most of my officers this morning, from Cape Francois, having been captured off Cape Tiberoon, on the 27th ultimo, by *La Concorde*, French frigate, mounting fifty-four guns, but pierced for fifty, after a chase of three hours.

Having seen the day before a superior force to windward, I judged it proper in compliance with your orders, to shift my station further to the westward; and on the morning of the 27th, I bore away to the northward under Cape Tiberoon, the weather being very squally, with much rain and a heavy sea. About half-past eleven o'clock, a.m., it clearing up a little, we perceived a large ship to the north-westward, to whom I made the private signal, but on its not being answered, I made sail to the south-east, in order to avoid her and get into the sea breeze to the southward of Tiberoon. But being baffled by the frequent shifts of wind, and the heavy sea running, we carried away the larboard fore-topmast studdingsail boom, and were obliged to cut away the lower and topmost studdingsails; on which I hauled across her (the frigate being then within gunshot) to the south-west and set the starboard foremast studdingsail; but a squall of wind coming on, carried away the fore-topgallant mast, and with it one man who was lost overboard.

The enemy now coming up very fast, and, though under her plain sails, sailing much faster than the *Hyaena*, I ordered all the guns that would bear from the starboard quarter to be fired at her, which she returned by firing some guns from her waist, and this gave us an opportunity of seeing her broadside. Soon after this, falling almost calm, and she bringing the breeze up alongside – the enemy's force being so much superior – I consulted my officers respecting our situation, who were unanimous in my opinion, that there was not a possibility of getting clear, nor had the *Hyaena* the least chance in fighting against such unequal force; when, after firing a few guns, and to save the effusion of blood, I judged it proper to surrender at about two o'clock. We found the *Concorde* to mount twenty-eight eighteen pounders on the maindeck, and to have 360 men on board.

We were taken on board the *Concorde*, and arrived at Cape François the 11th instant, after cruising against the English trade in company with the *Jupiter*, 74, and *Inconstant*, 36 guns. After our arrival we were kept prisoners on board until the 18th, when myself and officers were suffered to go on shore on parole, under the restriction of being mustered at our respective lodgings three times a day.

On the 20th June, the disputes commenced between the shipping and commissaries, which eventually laid the town in ashes – myself and the officers escaping to the beach through the fire of both parties, and most of us were obliged to swim off to the vessels for our lives, not one saving any part of their clothes or anything of value.

Hargood, with typical brevity in his statement to the officer in Jamaica, gives little indication of the horrors he had seen in San Domingo. The western part of the island, lying to the south-east of Cuba, is now Haiti. Nor does he mention how fortunate he was to be one of the few white men on the island to escape from it alive.

The prisoners were unfortunate enough to have been landed there just as the black slaves, incited by the French Revolutionaries, turned on the landowners of the sugar plantations in a particularly barbarous way. The population of San Domingo at that time numbered approximately 30,000 white inhabitants, and 24,000 free mulattoes, together with 480,000 black slaves who had been imported to the island to work on the sugar plantations, a source of enormous wealth.

In France the National Assembly had passed the Declaration of

Rights which stated that 'all men are born and continue free and equal as to their rights'. This was aimed partly at causing disaffection in San Domingo so that money from the plantations [removed from private ownership] could be seized by the Revolutionary Government in France. The news, spread by insurgents throughout the islands, promised freedom to people who, in many instances, were exploited and ill-used. On 23 August 1791 the slaves rose in rebellion and about 2,000 white people were massacred in the next two months. The negroes were joined by the mulattoes and the main harbour town of Port au Prince [now in Haiti]was burnt.

This gave a reason for the National Assembly to send commissioners from France to settle the colony. Two of the three who came, being members of the Revolutionary party, induced the slaves to fight by bribing them with pardons for all previous crimes and the promise of the sack of the town. Subsequently on the evenings of 19, 20 and 21 June the black troops entered Cape Town [now Port au Prince] and pillaged and destroyed all in sight. They turned on the white people without mercy; in one instance up to 300 people were burnt alive. Some tried to swim out to the French ships lying at anchor in the Bay, but were shot at in the water.

In the massacre the negroes fired alike upon whites and mulattoes. The white men defended themselves bravely, but they were all killed, not one being left in the town, though between 1200 and 1500 saved themselves by gaining the ships.

Such was the scene from which William Hargood was fortunate enough to escape.[1] One of his midshipmen [later Lieutenant Casey], who was not so lucky, recounted his own adventures and gave a succinct account of all that had occurred:

'On the night previous to the capture, this young officer dreamt that the *Hyaena* was taken by a large frigate painted black, and that he was carried prisoner to a place never before known to him, but which afterwards corresponded perfectly with the town of Cape François. At breakfast the next morning, he related the dream to his messmates, who laughed at him and endeavoured to drive the subject from his mind. Shortly before noon [however] his dream was fully borne out by the approach of the *Concorde*, just such a frigate as he had described to his messmates

'After our arrival at Cape François, and while arranging for our landing, the republican authorities on shore intimated that the warrant officers, mates, and midshipmen, should go to prison with the crew; insisting that by the French regulations, they were not entitled to their parole. Captain Hargood, on being made acquainted with this determination, opposed it most strenuously, and declared that if such were the case, he and all his officers would accompany them to prison – all should share alike. This noble and spirited conduct of our captain, who was backed by the captain of the *Concorde*, and the other French naval commanders in the harbour, who all appeared indignant, had the desired effect, and we were accordingly landed on our parole, but obliged to take up our residence in three different parts of the town: Captain Hargood and the gunroom officers in one place, the mates and midshipmen in another; and the warrant officers, and a youngster (the late Captain W.W. Daniels) and myself, in a distant part towards the west end.

'We had been in this new situation only a few days, when the town – one of the largest and finest in the West Indies – was attacked by a very large army of rebel blacks, setting fire to the different parts as they proceeded through the town, and indiscriminately shooting and murdering all the whites they met. The screams of men, women, and children were loud and dreadful; in fact the horrors of the scene can never be sufficiently described. Our lodgings were repeatedly forced open by armed drunken and infuriated blacks, and, in spite of their officers, my comrades and self were frequently threatened, and on the point of being put to death, and on several occasions were saved by the humane exertions of the black woman who owned the house in which we were lodged.

'This good woman, and her black female servants, appeared to have great influence with the insurgents; and once, when I was on the point of being put to death by a new party (for they were continually changing), she had to beg my life on her knees, and had great difficulty in succeeding. Such was this good woman's care and anxiety about us that she would scarcely leave us for a moment, and when obliged to do so, she left us in the care of her female servants, who were equally humane.'

Because of their being quartered at the west end of the town Brian Casey and his fellow midshipmen did not have a chance to swim out to the ships. Instead they were moved to the principal black

55

encampment a few miles from the town where they were kept in appalling conditions, with no cover from the wind and rain and only little and very bad food. Eventually they were brought back to a barracks in the town where they caught a sickness of which the gunner [of the *Hyaena*] died. Finally, however, they were released. Casey reached Jamaica, while the others got back to England.

Hargood who had managed to swim out to the *Concorde*, describes what happened thereafter:

> On my return to the *Concorde* I made known our situation to the Commander-in chief, who, with the Governor, said that as the town was destroyed, all order at an end on board the fleet, and no further communication was to be had with the National Commissaries, [that] they conceived our parole of honour done away, and that I might embark with my officers on board the caravel and proceed to Jamaica, without our any longer being considered prisoners of war. The morning before I sailed, I was informed that the boatswain, gunner, carpenter, and two midshipmen [one being Brian Casey] . . . had been made prisoners by the mulattoes, and marched into the country to the commissaries.

The capture of the *Hyaena* by the French was obviously a *cause célèbre* at least in naval circles at the time. Allen, writing nearly fifty years later, felt that he could not pass over an affair which at the time had threatened to ruin Hargood's career.

> It is far from the object of this work to enter upon any controversial matter, or to state anything which might give rise to the slightest dispute; but at the same time we feel bound to notice the version of this action afforded by James's Naval History.

Reading between the lines, it seems evident that Schomberg, like an evil genius, was once again attempting to influence the Lords of the Admiralty against people in any way connected with Prince William, who he so fervently disliked. Now a Post Captain, so in touch with the Navy Board, he appears to have been intent on getting his revenge on the Prince by defaming Hargood, who he knew to be his friend. Allen proceeds to explain what then occurred:

After quoting Captain Schomberg's account of the capture, in which it is incorrectly stated that the *Hyaena* sustained a severe and spirited conflict, in which she was much shattered, with several of her crew killed and wounded, Mr James gives his own remarks as follows:-

'The *Hyaena* being a ship of no more than 522 tons, mounting twenty-two long nine-pounders on her maindeck, and two long six-pounders, and six or eight ill-constructed useless carronades – twelve pounders – on her quaterdeck and forecastle, with a complement (she being on the peace establishment) of only 120 men and boys (this is a misstatement: the *Hyaena* had not one hundred men on board during the action; her second lieutenant with several men being absent in a prize) while the *Concorde* was a regular French 40-gun frigate, mounting 44 guns in all, *an obstinate resistance, on the part of the former, would have reflected the highest honour on the officers and crew of the British vessel* but *unfortunately* Captain Schomberg's account is erroneous in all the more important particulars. The circumstances of the case were these:-

'On the 27th May, early in the morning, when about two miles off Cape Tiberoon, the *Hyaena* was discovered and chased by the *Concorde*, the advanced frigate of a French squadron, composed of the *Eole* and *America*, 74s, three or four frigates, some of which then, or very soon afterwards, were in sight from the *Hyaena's* masthead. As soon as she discovered the character of her pursuers, the *Hyaena* put before a light air of wind, but being unable to make way against a heavy head sea, was rapidly gained upon. As the *Concorde* approached her on the quarter, the *Hyaena* fired a few of the main-deck guns, and then without waiting, it would appear, to receive any fire in return, hauled down her colours to the French frigate.'

Then follows a rebuke levelled at Sir William Hargood's neglect in not transmitting promised particulars of the action, as the cause of some misstatements in his first edition; and at some subordinate in a public office who disobeyed his chief by not furnishing him (Mr James) with full extracts from the official documents.

The remarks which seem to call most for a reply are given in italics; and with reference to the implied censure on the officers and crew who did not 'offer an obstinate resistance', it will, perhaps, be most advisable to give the opinion of as brave and good a seaman as ever commanded a British ship – the late Sir Thomas Hardy, in reference to a captain's duty in such cases.

It is given in Captain Hall's fragments, as a commentary upon the obstinate retreat, in a gale of wind, of a French privateer from a fast sailing frigate.

Sir Thomas Hardy's remark is stated to have been as follows:-

'This Frenchman's conduct may teach us the important lesson that an officer should never surrender his ship, whatever may be the forces opposed to him, WHILE THERE REMAINS THE SLIGHTEST POSSIBLE CHANCE OF ESCAPE.' And to this criterion the most fearless appeal may be made. The 'slightest possible chance of escape' did not remain to the *Hyaena*. It is indeed possible that by an 'obstinate resistance' Captain Hargood might have wantonly sacrificed blood, much too precious to be wasted, but to escape was impossible. The *Hyaena* was lying almost becalmed, while the *Concorde*, sailing three feet to her one, was bringing up a fine breeze. To have received the frigate's broadside would have been utterly useless in every sense of the word. He had no means of resistance at all adequate to the force opposed to him; and therefore, with a discretion which, in this instance, most certainly was the better part of valour, he sacrificed his own feelings to the good of the service and of his ship's company.

The following pages will afford full satisfaction to all, of the intrepidity of their subject, and we therefore dismiss the capture of the *Hyaena*, fully satisfied that no blame whatever can reasonably accrue to the memory of Captain Hargood for his conduct on this occasion.

The letter of Captain Hargood contains all the information relative to the circumstances attending to his release and that of his officers. The following were the captains who assembled to try him for the loss of the *Hyaena*:

On the 11th October 1793, a court martial, consisting of the following officers, assembled on board his Majesty' ship, *Cambridge*, in Hamoaze: viz :-

President – Rowland Cotton Esq., Rear-Admiral of the White, and Commander in chief at Plymouth.

CAPTAINS

George Bowen.	John Aylmer.
Richard Boger.	Francis Pender.
Herbert Sawyer.	Edward Buller.
George B. Westcott.	Charles Boyle.

H.M. Stokes Esq., Deputy Judge Advocate.

The court, in pursuance of an order from the Lords Commissioners of the Admiralty, dated 4th instant, directed to Rowland Cotton Esq, &c. &c., being first duly sworn, proceeded to inquire into the cause and circumstances attending the capture of his Majesty's late ship, *Hyaena,* by *La Concorde*, French frigate, on the 27th May last, off Cape Tiberoon; and to try Captain William Hargood, then commander of the *Hyaena*, his officers and crew, for their conduct on that occasion.

After hearing the evidence adduced, the court came to the following unanimous decision:-

The court is of opinion that everything was done that could have been done, by Captain William Hargood, his officers, and crew, to save his Majesty's ship *Hyaena* from being captured by the said frigate; and doth therefore most honourably acquit the said Captain William Hargood, his officers, and crew for the loss of the *Hyaena*: and they are hereby most honourably acquitted accordingly.

8

MUTINY

Six months after the court martial, on 13 April 1794, the members of the Board of the Admiralty showed their confidence in Captain Hargood by giving him the command of the 32-gun frigate *Iris*. The *Iris* was stationed in the North Sea to convoy the Baltic traders to and from Elsinore. Hargood remained in this somewhat monotonous service, enduring both cold and rough seas, for ten months until, in February 1795, he was transferred to take charge of the African convoy.

Accordingly, on the 5th February, he sailed from the Nore, and on the 16th joined Vice-Admiral Sir Hyde Parker, with the convoy in the Channel, in whose company he continued until the 2nd of March, when, being considered clear of the enemy's squadrons, the *Iris* and her convoy parted company from the Admiral, and arrived at Teneriffe on the 6th.

After taking on board wine at Teneriffe, Captain Hargood proceeded to Cape Coast, where he arrived with his convoy in safety on the 6th April. After running along the coast collecting freight, he directed his course homeward; and on the 24th May, being then in latitude 6°50"N. longitude 30°0"W., fell in with a French squadron of seven ships.

On discovering these ships the *Iris* stood towards them, and at four o'clock in the afternoon was near enough to make out the force of the strangers, which appeared to be one 50-gun ship on two decks, two frigates, two brigs, and two armed merchant ships.

The *Iris* having cleared for action stood towards the strangers, and at a quarter-past four made the private signal, which remained unanswered. Being at that time within random shot, one of the frigates and the two brigs hauled out to meet the *Iris*, and one of the brigs hoisted a red and white flag. The *Iris* soon afterwards commenced firing at the nearest brig, upon which she wore and joined her consorts to leeward; and the whole having declined to follow the *Iris* to action, bore away in form.

What this squadron really was it is now difficult, if not impossible, to ascertain; and the cause of this singular shyness on the part of the French commodore – for little doubt remained in the mind of Captain Hargood that it was a French squadron – cannot now be discovered; but the conduct of Captain Hargood in endeavouring to draw some of the ships after him, which he might attack with a prospect of success, was both skilful and admirable.

The *Iris* reached Spithead on 27 June, without meeting any other adventures, having on board a quantity of gold dust for freight.

Captain Hargood, still commanding the *Iris,* then sailed to Quebec. Returning from there with a large convoy he arrived at the Downs on the 4th December.

The *Iris* was then overhauled at Sheerness, after which Hargood continued to sail with her, escorting convoys in the North Sea, until, on the 23rd July 1796, he was superseded by Captain Thomas Surridge.

On the 14th August, 1796, Captain Hargood took command of the 50-gun ship *Leopard*, then lying off the Little Nore. The *Leopard* was for a time employed in convoying the Baltic and North Sea trade, for which Captain Hargood's extreme carefulness and attention eminently qualified him, although no service could be more disagreeable.

While the ship continued thus actively and continually employed, all went well, and a better ship's company could not be desired; but in the spring of 1797, the *Leopard* was ordered to join Vice-Admiral Duncan's fleet, in the ships of which reigned the most mutinous spirit, which had been reared and fostered by evil advisers and the baneful habit of ship visiting.

A portion of the *Leopard*'s crew was not long in catching the infection. On the 16th March she arrived from a cruise in the

Channel, and joined Admiral Duncan then lying in Yarmouth Roads. On the 17th she sailed with the fleet on a cruise in the North Sea, and returned on the 25th April.

Joseph Allen describes the now famous mutinies which broke out first at Spithead and then at the Nore as 'a blot and a stain upon the annals of England, which can never be thoroughly effaced'. In fact later and more enlightened historians are almost universally agreed in saying that the most surprising thing about the insurrection was that it had not happened before.[1]

The men's complaint that their pay was too small was totally justified. It had not been increased since Samuel Pepys had been Secretary to the Admiralty in 1661. At that time a wage of 22s.6d. a month (net after deductions) had been reasonable enough, but inflation had gradually reduced its worth. Moreover, merchant seamen, particularly in time of war, earned a great deal more. Then, to add insult to injury, soldiers' pay was increased to a shilling a day, in addition to which a sailor, on becoming a pensioner at Greenwich Hospital, got only half as much money as his military counterpart in Chelsea Hospital received.

The food meted out to the crews, although probably as much if not more than many of them would have got at home, was nonetheless very sub-standard. The mutineers' request for vegetables shows how they craved for something fresh.

Another great cause of grievance was the lack of shore leave. Men often spent years at sea. This had increased for two reasons. Firstly, during the American War of Independence ships had begun to be copper-bottomed, thus making it unnecessary to put into port so frequently for barnacles to be scraped from their hulls. Secondly, the very real probability that the men might take the chance to desert provided an added excuse for keeping then on board. The frequency of this happening was largely the result of the strictness of the discipline, and more especially the ferocity of the punishments which the unfortunate men were forced to undergo.

The most common chastisement, for almost any kind of crime, was that of a flogging with the cat-o'-nine-tails. Men seen to be slow in their work were beaten. The captain liked to see his sails hoisted quickly and a topman who got a rope stuck in a cleat was not spared. The 'cat' was a short wooden stick, covered with red baize. The tails were of tough knotted cord, about two feet long. The 'thieves' cat' had longer and heavier tails, knotted throughout their length. Only the captain could give the order to have a man flogged. He was not supposed to give more than twelve strokes but some sadists gave more. Most of the punishment was for drunkenness, the commonest crime on board ship.

The master–at–arms reported the miscreants to the first lieutenant who passed on their names to the Captain every morning. At six bells, or eleven o'clock, the Captain came on deck with a paper listing the names of the transgressors. The first lieutenant, told to summon all hands to witness the punishment, sent a midshipman to the boatswain's mates and the order was piped and shouted throughout the ship. The carpenter and his mates then dragged aft two of the wooden gratings which covered the hatches. One was laid flat on the deck, the other placed upright and secured. The Captain then called forth the first offender, told him he had transgressed the service and asked him if he had anything to say to excuse himself. On the man remaining silent he was told to 'strip' and, having taken off his shirt, his hands were tied to the upright grating by the quartermasters. The Captain then read the rule which the man had broken from the Articles of War, sweeping off his cocked hat as he did so in deference to the King. While this was happening one of the boatswain's mates produced the 'cat' and the hideous punishment began. One blow was enough to take off the skin. After twelve a man's back was like raw meat.

It was an inhuman punishment, unjustified even by the standards of the time. Yet those convicted of offences such as striking an officer endured the even greater and more prolonged torture known as 'flogging through the fleet'. The accused was put into the ship's longboat, his hands tied to a capstan bar. First he received several strokes of the 'cat' from a boatswain's mate. Then the boat was rowed away to the sound of the half-minute bell, the oars keeping time with the drummer who, sitting beside the victim, beat the rogue's march. The beatings were repeated as the boat rowed from ship to ship. Those who survived were washed with brine and treated with salves by the surgeon, but the torture was so dreadful that few came through it alive.

Other punishments included running the gauntlet, usually the fate of thieves. The crew formed a double line round the main deck, each man grasping a 'nettle', three tarry rope yarns twisted up and knotted at the end. The thief, stripped to the waist, was brought to the end of the line. The master-at-arms, with a drawn sword, confronted him, while two ship's corporals had their swords pointed at his back. A boatswain's mate first gave him a dozen lashes with the 'cat', after which he was forced to walk between the double line of men who gave him a whack with their nettles as he passed. After running the gauntlet a man, if he survived, was cleared of his offence. It was never mentioned again. Only the memory of what he had suffered remained, like the scars on his body, in his mind.

It must, however, be remembered that this was a violent age. There were stubborn, brutal and mutinous sailors, men whom magistrates had been only too glad to send to sea. Also men were brought aboard by the dreaded 'press gangs' which, particularly in coastal areas, spread terror throughout the land. This method of recruitment involved a party of seamen, led by a lieutenant, who descended on inns and cottages and even dragged men off the street to serve in His Majesty's ships.

As the French war started everything was done to induce men to volunteer. Some came forward, but still the Navy was short of hands. By 1795 Britain had one hundred and fifteen ships of the line and seventy-five thousand seamen. But even this was not enough. A first-rate ship like the *Victory* carried a crew of nearly a thousand. Everything depended on manpower, for, particularly during an action, a warship without a full compliment could not be efficiently manned.

In 1795 Pitt's government, facing a crisis as the French threatened to invade, passed the Quota Act. This impelled civil authorities to send a specified number of men from every county and town. In addition it became legal for foreigners to enlist. A man's nationality was unimportant so long as he was physically strong. The result was a new influx of jail birds, vagrants and immigrants, most of them resentful and some actively seditious. Many of these men, once accustomed to the discipline of the better-run ships, made good sailors, but others, inflamed by the tenets of the French Revolution, were insurgents who spread disruption through the fleet.

The sailors liked what they termed 'a smart captain'. Otherwise, in cases where surveillance was slack, the men themselves were persecuted by their more disreputable mates. Captains, therefore, of necessity had to be disciplinarians, but some, who would seem to have been in the minority, were humane.

Collingwood was the prime example of a commander who, by

sheer force of his personality, kept his crew under control. This was the man who swore, by the god of war, that a man should salute a reefer's (midshipman's) coat even if it was only merely hung up to dry. Yet he detested flogging, using it only on persistent offenders as a last resort. His system was proved to work, for his men respected him to the point that his ship was run with the efficiency of a well-oiled machine. Nelson, when confronted with hardened sinners, would say, 'Send them to Collingwood. He will tame them, if no one else can!'[2]

Hargood used the 'cat' only to punish persistent miscreants. His misfortune, when in command of the *Leopard*, was to find himself confronted with unforeseen and previously unknown circumstances over which he had little or no chance of control.

The mutiny at Spithead ended peacefully, thanks to the inter-vention of Lord Howe, known as 'Black Dick', and regarded as the sailor's friend. Howe, now ill and semi-retired, was living at Bath. Nonetheless, being still officially Commander-in Chief, he returned to replace the incompetent Lord Bridport (younger brother of Samuel, Lord Hood) and to visit every ship at Spithead. As a result of his report the Admiralty forced a frightened Parliament to pass an Act by which the ordinary seaman's pay was raised to 5s. 6d. a month. The mutiny, which in retrospect seems to have been fully justified, thus ended without bloodshed.

Hardly had this happened, however, when a much more dangerous disturbance broke out among the crews of ships which were lying at anchor in the mouth of the Thames at the Nore.

The mutiny at Spithead had already broken out when the *Leopard* returned from the North Sea. She then lay at anchor in Yarmouth Roads until, on the 14th May, her sailors rose in revolt.

At eight o'clock at night part of the ship's company assembled on the forecastle and gave three cheers; this unusual proceeding of course instantly brought the captain and every officer in the ship on deck. One man named George Burdon [obviously the ringleader] was seized and confined till the next morning . . . With much determination – although he had too much reason to fear the entire disaffection of his crew – Captain Hargood, at nine o'clock on the following morning, turned the hands up and punished George Burdon with a dozen lashes for the part he had taken on the preceding night; and it is possible that had not the *Leopard* remained in the company of ships the crews of which were so badly disposed, good order might have been quickly re-established.

On the 27th May the fleet put to sea at Lowestoft and then the mutiny broke out in its full force. The ship's companies took command of the ships from the captains and officers, and deserted the Admiral in great numbers. The conduct of Captain Hargood at this trying moment was of the most determined kind.

Admiral Duncan himself, in the *Adamant*, escaped from the turmoil into the open sea. The officers of the other ships apparently made little resistance except for Hargood on the *Leopard* and Trollope on the *Glatton*:

> Captain Hargood, of the *Leopard*, who, upon the mutineers putting the helm a-weather to take the ship into Yarmouth Roads, seized the wheel to prevent it, but was overpowered by them, and carried in their arms to his cabin.

Sir Charles Cunningham, who recorded this episode in a private memorandum, adds that, whereas Trollope had commanded the *Glatton* for some years, 'Captain Hargood had not held command of the *Leopard* for more than nine months, in the course of which he had been favoured with no such chance of gaining a hold upon the hearts of his ship's company.'[3]

The fact that they did not molest him, however, small man that he was, indicates that the burly seamen who carried him struggling to his cabin bore him no personal grudge. Once there, helpless and incensed with rage, he had to endure imprisonment for four interminable days.

> The *Leopard*'s mutinous crew put in to Yarmouth Roads on the 31st May where Captain Hargood was landed, but without the accompaniment of personal violence resorted to in many instances.
>
> On the 1st June the ship's company, having full possession of the ship, punished three men for drunkenness [by flogging,

one must presume]. The *Leopard* sailed on the 5th and arrived at the Nore on the 6th June, where she joined the rebellious Parker.

Richard Parker, dismissed from the Navy as a midshipman, had thereafter become bankrupt. Nonetheless, having some education, he had worked as a schoolmaster for a time. Returning to the Navy as an ordinary seaman, perhaps at the instigation of insurgents, he had established his Floating Republic at the Nore. A rabble-raiser extraordinary, he harangued the sailors, inciting them to rebellion, to the point where he had to suck lozenges to ease his throat!

Incensed by what he told them, his listeners rose in revolt. Gangs of men roamed the streets of Portsmouth. The mouth of the Thames was virtually blockaded, so that for some time most of the traffic of the Port of London virtually came to a halt. People became panic-stricken. Rumour ran wild that 'The Terror' which had transfixed France was about to begin. The government, in a state of near panic, called in the army. Doctor James McGrigor, [later to become Wellingon's Surgeon General] then surgeon of the 88th Regiment, the Connaught Rangers, gives an eye-witness account of what he saw:

'On our arrival in Portsmouth we found a great body of troops and everything in a most critical state on board the fleet, the officers having been sent on shore and the crew's delegates ruling everything. Great numbers of the sailors were on shore, roaming the streets and the neighbouring country in a mutinous and drunken state, their language and conduct most insubordinate and treasonable. At this time it was not thought prudent to interrupt them much; in fact a great part of the inhabitants of Portsmouth and its neighbourhood, and all the owners of public houses and of slop shops, with the dissolute females of the town, appeared to be of their party.'[4]

On the 7th June, [the day after the *Leopard* reached the Nore,] by order of Parker, the effigies of Mr Pitt and Mr Dundas [Secretary of War] were hung on the foreyardarms of the several ships, the crew of the *Leopard*, at the same time, firing great guns and muskets. This hanging in effigy on board the ships, caused the most painful sensation on shore, as it was considered that some of the officers were suffering.

Hargood did not return to the *Leopard*, but her story is well worth the telling, if only to record the courage and loyalty of her officers and some of her crew:

On the evening of the 10th of June Lieutenant Joseph Robb, with the help of two men called Russell and Moore, both master's mates, and several of the ordinary seamen, took advantage of a favourable wind and flowing tide. The mates succeeded in cutting the cables, the sails were loosed by a few of the men, and the ship deserted her bad cause.

The struggle was for a time very fierce, for several of the mutineers having got possession of the tops fired upon the officers and men on deck as long as their ammunition lasted; while another party rushed forward to the galley, and endeavoured to point two of the foremost guns aft. The spirited and gallant exertions of the officers and marines, however, quickly overpowered them; but in the conflict Mr I.Buchanan, master's mate, was mortally, and one marine, Charles Cubit, severely wounded.

As soon as the motions of the *Leopard* were seen on board the *Sandwich*, that ship and many others opened their fire upon her; but she succeeded in getting round the buoy of the Nore without injury and made sail up the Thames. By this time the greater part of the ship's company had joined the officers and assisted in making sail – the fire of the *Sandwich* still continuing. At a quarter before seven the ship got aground on the Middle Bank, but fortunately she was by that time out of gunshot.

Under these circumstance – the ship having no pilot on board – the commanding officer of the *Leopard* sent a boat to board two merchant brigs, and pressed the masters out of them as pilots. In another quarter of an hour the tide floated the ship off, and at eleven she anchored in Lower Hope, and secured nineteen of the ringleaders of the mutiny. The next day the *Leopard* again weighed, and proceeded further up the river, when a cutter came alongside and took eighteen of the mutineers out of the ship.

Thus was discipline once more restored; and in a very short time the just sentence of a court martial was carried into effect on Richard Parker . . . and on the 10th July four of the deluded crew of the *Leopard* also suffered the extreme penalty of the law on board that ship.

The *Leopard* had not been a happy ship for Hargood and two days later, on 12 July, Captain Thomas Surridge succeeded him in her command. Hargood meanwhile was appointed to the 64-gun ship *Nassau*.

On proceeding to take command of the *Nassau*, lying at the Nore, Captain Hargood was accompanied by Rear-Admiral Skeffington Lutwidge, who read His Majesty's pardon to all the ship's company except three, who had been delegates or members of the committee of the Floating Republic with Parker as their president. In the course of a few days, however, the royal pardon was extended to all the ship's company; and on the 22nd July, Captain Hargood sailed in the *Nassau* to reinforce Vice-Admiral Duncan's fleet off the Texel.

In order the more completely to re-establish good discipline on board the ships of this fleet – nearly all of which had been concerned in the mutiny – and also to watch the movement of the Dutch fleet, which had latterly given some indications of an intention to come out, the fleet continued cruising off the Texel for several months, notwithstanding it had to contend with much bad weather.

On the 10th September, in a heavy gale of wind, the *Nassau* strained so much that it was found necessary to keep the lee chain pumps going and she also sprung her bowsprit. But Captain Hargood made no report of the defects of his ship while there was a prospect of sharing in an action with the Dutch.

Therefore she continued to cruise with Admiral Duncan until the end of September, at which time the whole fleet bore up to Yarmouth for provisions. Here, on the *Nassau*'s defects becoming known to the Admiral, Captain Hargood was ordered to proceed to the Nore, where he arrived on the 10th October, the day preceding that on which was fought the battle of Camperdown.

The victory on that day conferred the highest honour on the gallant Duncan, especially when it is considered that the men under him who then worked the guns in defence of their country, had, only a few months previously, turned the same guns against their officers.

The *Nassau* did not go to sea again while Captain Hargood commanded her, but remained as a guardship at the Nore and in the river Thames.

For Hargood himself, the news of Duncan's triumph although welcome, must have deepened his despondency produced by the recent events. Marooned in the Thames, he must surely have felt that the Navy held little future for him and that he had reached the nadir of his career. Little could he guess how soon new opportunities would arise and that within the space of only a few months his fortunes would greatly change.

FAR EASTERN SEAS

On the 23rd February, 1798, Captain Hargood took command of the 64-gun ship *Intrepid*, in the Downs, and on the 30th April sailed for the East Indies, having under convoy ten sail of ships belonging to the East India Company, and two store-ships. On the 6th July he arrived at Rio de Janeiro, and sailed from thence to China direct, arriving at Macao on the 16th November. The *Intrepid* sailed from Macao for Anson's Bay, China, and having seen her convoy safe, returned to Macao.

While working into Lintin Bay – owing to the obstinacy of a Chinese pilot who was on board, and who persisted in standing on, notwithstanding Captain Hargood's remon-strances – the *Intrepid* took the ground. She was got off again without much damage; but some of the leading of the stem being damaged, one of the crew, an expert diver, volunteered to go down under her bottom and nail it on; and this was effected much to the satisfaction of all on board.

The First Coalition against the French had now dissolved. Prussia, determined to annexe Poland, had been the first to leave. Then Spain, having made peace with France, was now fighting on her side. Her ships, like those of the French, were better designed and sailed faster than those of the British. The advantage which this gave, however, was outmatched by the poor calibre of her officers which resulted in less efficient crews. Their gunners in particular were slower and less efficient than those on the British ships. Moreover, the policy of her senior naval officers, in common with those of the French, was to avoid all open conflict if any alternative could be found.

While lying at Macao, in company with the 74-gun ship *Arrogant*, Captain George Oliver Osborn, and 38-gun frigate *Virginie*, Captain George Astle, Captain Hargood had an opportunity of showing his skill in defending the ships under his orders from capture by a Spanish and French squadron of greatly superior force.

Hargood's official letter to the Secretary of the Admiralty describes in detail what occurred.

His Majesty's ship *Intrepid*,
in the Straits of Malacca,
February 25th, 1799.

'Sir,

I beg you will acquaint my Lords Commissioners of the Admiralty, that I wrote to them on the 12th December, 1798, then informing them of my reason for stopping in China, and that I purposed sailing on the 1st. February 1799, with the homeward-bound traders to see them clear of the China Seas. On the 21st January, his Majesty's ships *Arrogant*, Captain G.O. Osborn, and *La Virginie*, Captain Astle, arrived in Macao Roads, for the purpose of taking charge of the homeward-bound ships. The two ships arrived in great want of stores, water, &c., and *La Virginie* with the loss of her mizenmast. At the time of their arrival I was lying at Lintin, in his Majesty's ship under my command, having heard that there was a force fitting out at Manilla, intended for the coast of China; but in consequence of a letter I received from Captain Osborn, acquainting me that he purposed moving his ship to Samkoke, to water, leaving *La Virginie* near the Typa to get up a jury-mast, and water &c., and for the reason of being ready to sail on the day appointed, I judged it prudent to move to Samkoke [Samoke] also, which I did on the 25th January, at that time it blowing a hard gale from the northward which continued for several days.

On the morning of the 27th, I observed some ships coming round an island near us, with English colours flying; I immediately made the private signal, but finding it not answered, I concluded them to be ships belonging to the enemy. I lost no time in making Captain Osborn acquainted with it, and having a short time only to consider what was best to be done, I determined to cut or slip in order to afford protection to *La Virginie*, which was not less than three or four leagues from me, and also with a view to draw the enemy to sea, to give me an opportunity of engaging them after joining the frigate.

I am happy to say that my views were so far accomplished that the enemy followed us for several leagues, but did not choose to bring us to action. The Admiral when nearly in gunshot hauled to the wind, finding it was not in his power to cut off the frigate, as did the rest of the enemy's ships, which then worked to windward endeavouring to anchor, which some of them could not accomplish owing to the violence of the wind. I immediately hauled to the wind to endeavour to draw them into action, and also to regain the anchorage where I was to meet the convoy, then hourly expected down the river.

I beg to acquaint you that I saw nothing of the enemy after the 27th. The squadron consisted of six sail: viz. two line-of-battle ships – one an 80-gun ship with a flag at the mizen [sic] the other a 74 – and two frigates Spanish, the other two being French frigates. The weather continued very boisterous for several days, so that it was with difficulty I could regain my anchorage near Macao, but I at length effected it on the 2nd February, and continued to work up the river to join the convoy till the 5th, when having been joined by the convoy, I sailed on the 7th; and am happy to inform you that I fully succeeded in my wishes with regard to its protection.

I beg further to acquaint you, that from the sudden appearance of the enemy on the 27th, I was necessitated to cut my cables, as was also the *Arrogant,* and to leave what boats we had out. Upon my arrival at Malacca Roads with the convoy, I found orders from Rear-Admiral Rainier, dated 8th October and 5th November, directed to Captain Osborn, ordering the *Arrogant* and *La Virginie* to the Malabar coast.

I have the honour to be, &c.

W.Hargood.

E. Nepean Esq.,
Admiralty Office, London.

Don Ignacio de Alava, commander of the Spanish squadron, gave a rather different version of events. Little did he know when he

73

published the narrative of his proceedings in 1799 that his path was to cross that of Hargood under even more dramatic circumstances. Six years later his vice- admiral's flag would be flying from the masthead of the *Santa Ana* during her gargantuan struggle with Hargood's ship the *Belleisle*.

His account, as quoted by Allen, is headed as follows: -

A NARRATIVE OF THE PROCEEDINGS OF THE DIVISION WHICH LEFT MANILLA IN THE MONTH OF JANUARY OF THE PRESENT YEAR, 1799.

Don Ignacio de Alava, the Commander-in-Chief of the naval forces of Spain in Asia, sailed from Manilla Bay the 9th January, with the ships of the line *Europa* and *Montanes*, and the frigates *Lucia* and *Fama*, of the squadron under his command, and the French frigate and corvette *Preneuse* and *Brule Guelle*, on a cruise, which from circumstances could not exceed thirty or forty days. A few days after he had put to sea, being on his route to Canton, he examined a neutral vessel, whose captain informed him that the English convoy of ten Company's ships were getting ready with every expedition at Whampoa, and he thought would sail from the roads for Europe the 28th or 30th of the same month of January, under escort of the *Intrepid* ship of war, which was at anchor on the 10th at the island of Grand Lama, being the only ship of war at that period in China.

With this intelligence the Commander-in-Chief determined to cross over to that coast, so arranging it as to enter Macao Roads as nearly as possible on the day when he conceived the convoy would sail, for the purpose of attacking it below the Tigris [the Spanish writer must mean the mouth of the Yang-Tze-Kiang] where he supposed it would remain until the time of departure.

He [de Alava] communicated his ideas in the form of particular instructions addressed to the commanders of his ships; prescribed the manner in which he would make the attack, whether on the *Intrepid* alone, which was known to be arrived, or on her and the two frigates, *Fox* and *Carysfoot*, which had sailed from thence on the 10th December, but might be returned; or finally on those three ships and the *Victorious*, in the event of her being arrived, as was supposed and reported, with the above-mentioned two frigates, since the 10th January.

He [de Alava] shaped his course so that on the 26th (European reckoning) our division entered all in company among the islands of China by the Grand Lama, which he examined until he was well assured that no vessel was there as had been affirmed by the neutral vessel. Having interrogated various Chinese, who were received on board under the denomination of pilots, but more for the purpose of gaining intelligence than on any other account, he could only comprehend from their most strange language that the *Intrepid* had sailed a few days before with five Company's ships, that there were fifteen more at Canton, and that at Macao there was no English ship whatever. The same, with but small variations, was understood from their respective pilots by the commanders of the corvette *Brule Guelle*, and the frigate *Santa Lucia*, to whom the Commander-in-Chief had given it in charge to collect intelligence. This account was rendered so much the more probable from knowing that five Company's ships had sailed about the middle of January, and it appeared natural that the *Intrepid's* having taken a station at the most advanced island of the archipelago, could only be with the view of being ready for a sudden start. This being the case he considered the attempt fruitless; but neither on this, nor on account of the bad weather, which, with darkness, rain and heavy squalls from the northward, rendered the entrance very critical, did the Commander-in-Chief desist from it, but stood on gaining what he could until night fell, when, collecting his ships, he came into the channel of the Great Lantas, south-east a quarter south of the elevated mountain of the island.

The 27th, in the morning, at the beginning of the flood tide, he made the signal for sailing, notwithstanding the continuance of the northerly wind, with squalls, snow, and intense cold, which caused a great impression on the Europeans accustomed to a hot climate, but had such an effect upon the Indians that one of them died frozen at the foot of his gun. At half-past ten, a.m. the ship *Europa*, frigates *Preneuse* and *Santa Lucia*, and corvette *Brule Guelle*, reached the windwardmost island, but the *Montanes* and *Fama*, which were more to the southward, were obliged to make another small tack, which threw them considerably astern. At this time the *Brule Guelle*, which was somewhat ahead of the *Europa*, gave notice of her having discovered two ships bearing west-south-west, which were making signals, and from this he concluded they were ships of an enemy. We [the Spanish] immediately shortened sail to enable the sternmost ships to close, and instantly on opening a passage between two islands, descried in the roads two ships of war at anchor, distant about six or seven miles, and with private signals, which the Commander-in-Chief answered by hoisting flags at the mast-head, which, while they indicated to our ships the sight of an enemy, and directed the general attack in a body, would serve to confound the enemy, or put them in doubt respecting the agreement of the signals, the horizon being so dark that colours could not be distinguished.

Taking advantage of the opportunity to bring the second island in a line with the two enemy's ships, from whom by this means our movements were concealed, the Commander-in-Chief hove to, in order that the frigates *Santa Lucia* and *Preneuse*, which were coming up, might join, and the *Montanes* and *Fama*, which were far astern, might shorten their distance; but as the island which hid us from the enemy was of small extent, and it was necessary to conceal from them our motions, not to raise further suspicion, so it became necessary to proceed on before the last two mentioned ships joined, and to determine on coming to action with the *Europa*, *Preneuse*, and *Santa Lucia* (which had sailed under English colours) to the attack of the two ships. These made sail precipitately, slipping their cables, leaving all their boats and launches that they might not impede their way, and directing their course through the channel of the Grand Ladrone. The flagship repeated signals for the other, which was at anchor athwart her, to follow, and likewise for a large frigate of French construction, of fourteen guns of a side, which came out from another anchorage nearer Macao, to join the ships of the line. Being put to flight they displayed their English ensigns and pendants; and the Commander-in-Chief confirmed the Spanish flag by a shot directed at the sternmost, which was distant little more than two miles.

Such was the position of the ships at half-past twelve, when

76

we passed in sight of the castle and town of Macao. The frigates *Preneuse* and *Santa Lucia* continued to follow the *Europa*, which made all sail that the weather permitted; and although she gained upon the enemy she got much more ahead of the two frigates, and still more of the *Montanes*, which, with the *Fama*, was at two o'clock distant seven miles.

The Commander-in-Chief saw that with the *Europa* alone there was no probability of attacking with advantage two ships of the line that kept well together, and the frigate, which from her position could easily join them whenever the action might commence; that he could not come to a partial engagement with the *Victorious* [*Arrogant*]which appeared to be the sternmost ship; and that it was wholly impossible to cut off the frigate which kept in shoal water. Nevertheless he [de Alava] continued the pursuit of the enemy, with the precaution of keeping to windward of them, in order to prevent their falling upon him with the two ships and the frigate, and forcing the *Europa* out of the combat before she was reinforced, and by that means remain superior to the rest of the division.

Having gone on until we [the Spanish ships] had only the depth of one fathom below the keel, and at the rate of eleven or twelve miles an hour, in a place where the pilot said there was little water, and they would probably run aground, and that he deemed the continuance of the chase a great risk, the Commander-in-Chief determined to give it over, and hauled his wind on the starboard tack to collect his vessels.

Having accomplished this, and the wind by its strength being little governable, he gave the order for anchoring in seven fathoms, under shelter of the island Montana, at half-past four in the afternoon, directing a junction so necessary in sight of an enemy's force so little inferior to our own. The circumstances in which the *Montanes* and *Preneuse* were, at the instant when the *Europa* came to, obliged these ships to remain at a great distance to leeward, and in a situation subject to an attack under a great disadvantage by the enemy, who were distant three leagues to the southward, and had hauled their wind in an east-north-east course, steering for the island of the Grand Ladrone.

'On observing this, the Commander-in-Chief making the

signal for the *Montanes* not to come to, determined again to make sail and join, forming the line of battle on the larboard tack – the natural order. To this signal which was complied with at five o'clock, followed that of making known that it was his design to attack the enemy the next night if an opportunity offered, showing at the same time that he would steer a south-east course, which was their bearing at dark, and where he thought it most probable he should fall in with them, supposing that they would soon put about to steal away from us.

'At the close of the evening he determined the order of sailing with a gun, and steered the course appointed, with his topsails double reefed and lowered down. A few minutes after this, the commander of the *Montanes*, which followed the *Europa* in line, communicated to the Commander-in-Chief that he had sprung his mainyard, which made it impossible for him to make any effort whatever. This accident to the ship of the greatest force placed us in an inferiority to the enemy; for this reason, and that the wind and haze had so considerably increased as to prevent our distinguishing the two leading ships, and to render our motions and the interpretation of signals hazardous, it did not appear prudent to the Commander-in-Chief to engage in a new and fruitless chase, notwithstanding there were many of the crew who discerned the enemy's ships amidst the great obscurity which, as the Commander-in-Chief suspected, were on the opposite tack, without showing any light whatever.

'That they might not doubt of our position, and notwith-standing the tiers of all our ships were illuminated, he ordered the three poop lanterns to be lighted, and one at the masthead, that the other ships might do the same, and continue the course that had been fixed upon.

The design of the Commander-in-Chief was to take the former anchorage the two English ships had left, but the acci-dent to the mainyard of the *Montanes* did not permit it; and he had, therefore, to rest satisfied with seeing two English ships of the line and one frigate run and abandon the port before two Spanish ships of the line and three frigates, with whom they did not choose to measure their strength – not much less infe-rior than that of three Spanish gun-boats compared with two

English frigates whose Commodore* published last year, as a glorious achievement, their having taken a few vessels that went to the assistance of one in distress, and afterwards reconnoitring the Bay of Manilla, where he knew there was no ship in a state to be able to oppose him.
Manilla, 11h February, 1799.'

[Allen's narrative continues]

The best contradiction which can be offered to the bombast of the Spanish Commander-in- Chief was the fact that, so much disgusted was Captain L'Hermite, of the *Preneuse*, with the conduct of Rear-Admiral de Alava, that he withdrew his force from under his orders and refused to act any longer in concert with him. But there must be another point or two of the Spanish Admiral's account noticed: one is the assertion that at the time he considered it necessary to leave off the pursuit of the British ships, he had only one fathom under his keel; whereas the *Intrepid*, at the time when the *Europa* hauled her wind and declined to engage, was in ten fathoms! Mizen head bearing west south-west, distant six or seven leagues.

The accompanying comparative statement of the force of the respective squadrons will be a sufficient answer to the piece of effrontery which concluded the Spanish Admiral's apology:-

BRITISH	Guns	SPANISH AND FRENCH		Guns
Intrepid	64	*Europa*		80
Arrogant	74	*Montanes*		74
Virginie	<u>40</u>	*Preneuse*		36
Total	178	*Santa Lucia*		34
Spanish	<u>282</u>	*Fama*		34
Inferiority	<u>104</u>	*Brule Guelle*	<u>24</u>	<u>282</u>

* This piece of sarcasim is an allusion to the gallant and well-conducted attempt of Captains Edward Cooke and Pultency Malcolm in the *Sybille* and the *Fox* at Manila in January 1798.

The above is a mere random statement, but it will suffice to show the real disparity under which Captain Hargood was contented to meet his enemy; and although these facts have been long suffered to sleep unnoticed, it is not too late to bring them to light, in order that they may afford due testimony to his skill and bravery – skill in defeating the object of the Spanish Admiral by covering the detached frigate; and bravery in offering battle to a force so superior, when he had done so. The eminent service performed by Captain Hargood, was acknowledged in the subjoined letter from Rear-Admiral Rainier, the British Commander-in Chief.

Suffolk, off Mangalore,

24th April, 1799.

'Sir,

'I take the earliest opportunity to acknowledge the receipt of your letter dated Malacca Road, 23rd February last, which came to hand only the 16th instant, by his Majesty's ship *La Virginie*, at Bombay, giving an account of your proceedings, particularly in the instance of the attack attempted on the detachment of his Majesty's ships, then under your command, in Macao Road, on the 27th January last, by a very superior combined force of the enemy – Spanish and French, wherein your spirited and judicious conduct, in the pursuit of them, and fairly offering them battle, which they declined, merits my fullest approbation, particularly as it afforded you the opportunity of executing my orders, in conducting a most valuable convoy of East India ships through a most perilous navigation in safety; the intercepting thereof was, beyond a doubt, the grand object the enemy had in view.

I am. &c. &,
Peter Rainier.

W. Hargood, Esq.
Captain HMS *Intrepid*.

During the year 1801 the *Intrepid* frequently bore Sir Peter Rainier's flag, but for the most part continued to be actively employed in protection of convoys during the time she remained on the station. There is no event recorded of any particular interest until the year 1802, when, in the month of

1. Admiral Sir William Hargood, GCB, GCH. *(National Maritime Museum)*

2. *(left)* Captain Maurice
Suckling.
(National Maritime Museum)

3. *(below left)* Peter Rainier.
(National Maritime Museum)

4. *(below)* Captain Peter Parker
(National Maritime Museum)

5. *Belleisle,* fifteen minutes past noon, 21 October 1805. *(National Maritime Museum)*

6. *Belleisle* at 4pm. Ships from left to right: *Dumanoir, Naiad, Belleisle, Santa Ana, Victory, Achille.*

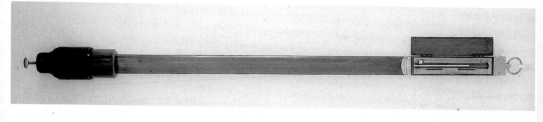

Victory July 1: 1805

My Dear Hargood

As the day is very fine I was in hopes that you would have come onboard and dined, from Winds, and the expectation of Wind I have been afraid to ask my friends to dinner, but I need not I hope apuse you how glad I am always to see you, being Dear Hargood Yours Most faithfully

Nelson & Bronte

Capt: Hargood

7. Nelson's letter to Hargood written with his left hand.

8. Hargood's barometer on the *Belleisle*.

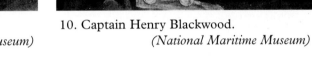

9. Rear Admiral Sir Horatio Nelson.
(National Maritime Museum)

10. Captain Henry Blackwood.
(National Maritime Museum)

11. Captain George Duff.
(National Maritime Museum)

12. Admiral Cuthbert Collingwood.
(National Maritime Museum)

13. Prince William, later
King William IV.
(National Maritime Museum)

14. Captain Sir William Hoste.
(National Maritime Museum)

15. The *Arrogant, Intrepid* and *Virginie* chasing a French and Spanish Squadron off the coast of China, 27 January 1799. *(National Maritime Museum)*

16. Napoleon Bonaparte being transferred from the *Northumberland* to the *Bellerophon* on his way to St Helena, 1815. *(National Maritime Museum)*

17. Miss Maria Somers Cocks, later wife of Admiral Sir Willliam Hargood.

18. Miss Margaretta Sarah Somers Cocks, later wife of Admiral Sir James Nicoll Morris.

March, Captain Hargood conveyed troops at a critical period – being preparatory to the Mahratta war – from Goa to Bombay and other parts of the coast. This service was warmly applauded by the Governor in council at Bombay, and also by the Governor General; and on his return to England Captain Hargood was presented with three hundred guineas by the Court of Directors of the India House.

Admiral Rainier forwarded a letter he had received from the Marquess Wellesley, brother of Wellington and at that time Governor General of India. Wellesley wrote from Fort William on 22 May 1802 : 'I have great satisfaction in acknowledging that Captain Hargood has rendered an essential service to the public, by the zeal and alacrity which he has manifested in complying with the request of the Government of Bombay, for the employing his Majesty's ships in the conveying British troops from Goa to Bombay.'

This seems to have been the conclusion of Captain Hargood's service in India, for the *Intrepid*, being in a very crazy state was ordered to England. She accordingly sailed from Madras on the 8th October, arrived at the Cape of Good Hope on 3rd December, and reached Spithead on the 14th February, 1803. The *Intrepid* was paid off at Chatham on the 5th April.

10

THE GREAT CHASE

This chapter is largely based on a first-hand account by
Lieutenant John Owen (later Adjutant-General) of the Marines.

The *Belleisle** was the ship in which William Hargood made his name in the annals of naval history.

> After having paid off the *Intrepid* he remained unemployed until the 23rd November in the same year, when he received his commission for the *Belleisle,* then in the Mediterranean; and he accordingly proceeded to join her, taking a passage out from England in a frigate.

The *Belleisle* had in fact been captured from the French ten years before. Sailors are always superstitious. It is said to be unlucky to give a ship a new name, so perhaps it was for this reason that it remained unchanged. Like most French-built ships she was well designed. A French 74-gun ship at the end of the 18th century was bigger, more roomy and sailed faster than her British counterpart.

Naval artists of the time have depicted the beauty of a ship of the line in full sail. Masefield, describing them, wrote, 'Viewed from without, a First, Second or Third rate wooden man-of-war appeared ponderous and cumbersome . . . But when the great sails were set, and the hull began to move through the sea, the cumbrous hulk took on attributes of beauty and nobility. There has been perhaps, no such

---

* Hargood's ship was called *Belleisle*. Off the north-west coast of France, south of Lorient, is the island of Belle Ile. Off the coast of Labrador, north of Newfoundland, is the island of Belle Isle. All rather confusing.

82

beautiful thing on earth, the work of man's hands, as an old 74 under sail.'[1]

It was not until the 18th March 1804, that Captain Hargood joined his ship, which was then cruising off Cape Sicié, as one of Nelson's fleet, blockading the French fleet in Toulon. This service was one demanding the most incessant watchfulness: and weeks, months, and almost years passed without the smallest alleviation.

The station generally preserved – half-way between the Capes Sicié and Cépet – was also exposed to the most sudden and disagreeable changes of weather, frequently making it requisite to close reef the topsails, and causing no slight loss in topmasts, topsail yards, &c.

The *Belleisle* had been in commission rather more than a year when Captain Hargood took command, superseding Captain John Whitby; and as she had been one of the most constant cruisers, her ship's company were suffered to have, by way of a treat, a run to Naples to procure refreshments for the fleet.

On the 25th March the *Belleisle* was ordered to part company, and on the 29th arrived in Naples Bay, where, having taken on board bullocks and refreshments of every kind, such as lemons, oranges, onions, &c., she sailed again on the 2nd April, and rejoined Lord Nelson on the 8th.

Lieutenant Owen, ultimately Adjutant-General of the Marines but now a young lieutenant serving under Hargood in the *Belleisle*, describes how, except for those three days at Naples, the *Belleisle* was for twenty-one months at sea. He remarks that, 'It is rather a curious fact that during that long period the officers were obliged to send their linen to be washed either at Malta or Gibraltar, a distance of not less than two hundred leagues.'

The *Belleisle* then cruised till the 11th May 1804, when she anchored with the fleet in Agincourt Sound, a deeply indented bay on the north coast of Sardinia. This anchorage was one particularly useful to Lord Nelson, before whose time it had, probably, seldom been used by a British cruiser. The harbour – which Lord Nelson pronounced the finest he had ever seen – was brought to light by Captain Ryves, of the 64-gun ship *Agincourt*, after which ship it was named. A cluster of small islands, known as the Maddalenas, sheltered the entrance to the sound, and formed an excellent breakwater. To this watering place the British ships frequently resorted, but their stay was as short as possible, never exceeding eight days, and seldom remaining for so long a time.

In the month of June the *Belleisle* was attached to the lee or inshore division of the fleet; and on the 13th and 14th formed one of the squadron which drove the French Admiral back into Toulon, from which port he was attempting a kind of sortie, or rather feint. Shortly afterwards a fleet of transports, under the convoy of the *Leviathan*, arrived, and the body of the fleet, with Lord Nelson, sailed with them to Palma Bay, Sardinia, to unload; leaving the charge of the station to Captain Hargood, in the *Belleisle*, with the frigates *Fisgard* and *Niger*, and *Acheron* bomb vessel.

On the 30th July and 1st of August, a violent gale of wind off shore, drove the squadron out to sea; and on the 2nd five sail of French line-of-battle ships and six frigates, commanded by Rear-Admiral Pelley, in the *Formidable*, made their escape out of port, and cruised in the neighbourhood until the 5th.

Captain Hargood had succeeded in the meantime, after having exerted all his powers to do so, in resuming his station, and on this day having got in sight of the telegraph upon Cape Cépet, the signal was made that his squadron consisted of six sail-of-the-line. To counteract this alleged force, the French *Neptune* stood out to the support of Rear-Admiral Pelley; but, notwithstanding the equality of force even according to the French mode of reckoning, M. Dumanoir le Pelley considered it advisable to retreat; and Captain Hargood, on approaching nearer the land, was enabled to distinguish the seven sail of French ships re-entering the harbour.

On the 8th Captain Hargood stood close to the shore, and counted the sail of the line, six frigates and a brig, at anchor in the outer roads. Lord Nelson did not return to his station until the 26th.

In the month of November Captain Hargood was ordered in shore under Cape Sebastian, with the *Belleisle* and two frigates, where he detained a large number of vessels, both Spanish and Austrian. The vacillating conduct of the Spanish government, and certain rumours which reached Lord Nelson, induced him to take this step, although instructions from the British government authorising him had not then arrived.

The *Belleisle*'s boats were in constant use boarding vessels; and as the matter turned out, Lord Nelson was only anticipating the orders then on their way from the Admiralty. Dispatches, dated the 19th September, reached him on the 25th December, directing him to take such precautionary measures as might appear necessary for counteracting or opposing any hostile attempts of the Spaniards against the British possessions or commerce; but he was restricted from any act of downright hostility, with the exception that he was to detain Spanish ships conveying treasure or military stores.

These orders were further qualified by the Admiralty in subsequent letters; but the caution was needless, for Spain was inveigled by France into joining her in the war against England, thereby adding another load to that which was already rapidly humbling that once proud country to the dust.

On the 14th December 1804, the declaration of war against England was signed at Madrid.

The force at the disposal of Lord Nelson at this critical period was only eleven sail of the line, and scarcely a frigate or sloop to send with dispatches. These ships too were all more or less in need of repair, and many scarcely seaworthy. In Toulon, at the commencement of the year 1805, were eleven sail of the line and seven frigates ready for sea; and on the declaration of war by the Spanish government, it became evident that a junction with the Spanish fleets in Carthagena, Cadiz, and Ferrol would be attempted. The Toulon fleet did accordingly – taking advantage of the temporary absence of the British blockading force at Agincourt Sound – put to sea on the 17th January, having on board 3,500 troops.

The British lookout ships were the *Active* and *Seahorse*, and these hastened with the intelligence to the Admiral, then watering his fleet at the aforementioned anchorage. Not a moment was lost by Lord Nelson in putting to sea with his small fleet, and all sail was made to get round Sardinia in search of the enemy; in doing which the fleet passed through the narrow channel separating the small island of Biche from the mainland, – a passage most intricate and beset by dangers.

Lieutenant Owen describes, how after the monotony of the blockade of Toulon, 'It may be conceived with what joy the officers and men received the intelligence communicated by signal from the *Seahorse* and *Active* frigates, "that the enemy's fleet had put to sea"'.

Owen continues to tell how 'The squadron was at that time watering in Agincourt Sound. It was three o'clock in the afternoon of a day late in January 1805. The water casks and boats were ordered on board, the fleet unmoored, and soon after dark was underway, running between some low rocky islands which form the eastern passage from the Sound; a very perilous manoeuvre, for the success of which Lord Nelson, next morning, publicly expressed his gratitude.'

On the 22nd January, at noon, the *Seahorse* rejoined, having fallen in, on the preceding day, with a French frigate off Pulla Bay, but Captain Boyle was unable to examine the anchorage owing to the heavy gale of wind then blowing and the thick weather. The *Seahorse* and *Active* were then ordered to Palma Bay and also to Cagliari, but without obtaining the smallest tidings.

Sardinia being, therefore, deemed safe, Lord Nelson departed for Naples, Palermo, and Messina, but still no news was obtained; and the Admiral then concluded in his own mind that the destination of the French fleet was the Morea or Egypt.

For the Morea and Egypt therefore the fleet sailed and on the 4 February arrived off Alexandria, and communicated with the Consul, but nothing had been heard there of the French fleet, writes Owen.

Every ship was ready for action at a moment's warning; all the bulkheads down fore and aft; and a fleet in better order for fight probably never floated. Though few the ships were united in one firm bond, each looking to their chief director, and anxious to anticipate his wishes and forward his views.

Never, perhaps, was the master spirit more universally acknowledged than it was in the person of Lord Nelson. Captains, officers, and men, alike felt that his judgement was correct and to be depended on; and such was the confidence his presence inspired that each would, fearlessly, have approached a force doubly superior, relying for victory upon Nelson's abilities and nautical wisdom.

Coron and Alexandria were visited; but no intelligence at all bearing upon the probable designs of the French could be obtained, and Nelson, half-mad with vexation, steered for Malta.

In the meantime, the French fleet which had given rise to such anxiety, was snug in Toulon; for on the second day after M.Villeneuve had quitted Toulon, his fleet, in crossing the Gulf of Lyons, encountered a heavy gale, in which many of his ships were greatly damaged, and one line-of battle ship – the *Indomptable* – and three frigates separated from him. The *Cornèlie* was one of the latter.

Lieutenant Owen tells how 'when we approached Malta, a frigate joined with the information that the enemy's fleet had returned to Toulon, having been damaged by the gales we had also experienced on leaving Sardinia.'

On the 27th February, Lord Nelson with his fleet – after his unsuccessful pursuit – anchored in Pulla Roads, where, having in the course of two days watered, he again attempted to put to sea to renew his search. After three attempts on three successive days, the persevering Admiral at length succeeded in working to the westward of Palma Bay; but a heavy gale came on, and forced the fleet to run for shelter to that anchorage.

It was not, therefore, till the 12th March, that the *Belleisle*, which had followed Nelson in all his wanderings, again arrived off Toulon; and on the 15th, the usual winter station off Cape Sebastian was reached; but a fleet of transports having arrived at Palma Bay, containing provisions and stores, of which the ships were greatly in want, Lord Nelson bore up, and on the 27th returned to that anchorage.

The French Vice-Admiral, having in the meantime refitted

his fleet, on learning the departure of the blockading fleet, again put to sea on the 30th. His departure was quickly observed by the British lookout frigates, *Active* and *Phoebe*, the latter of which instantly made all sail, with the welcome intelligence to Palma Bay. The fleet had shifted from Palma to Pulla Bay for the convenience of watering, and at this latter place the *Phoebe* found it.

'The *Pheobe*, joined with the welcome intelligence that the enemy was again at sea, and had steered to the westward,' wrote Lieutenant Owen.

The chase was renewed. Nelson sailed round Sicily without seeing a sign of the French fleet. Owen declares that 'from this time we had foul winds till we arrived at Tetuan, on the coast of Barbary, where we anchored to complete our stores, and learned that the enemy had passed the Streights (sic) of Gibraltar.'

Nelson did not reach Gibraltar until the 30th April 1805. The fleet, still impeded by contrary winds, anchored in Mazari Bay, [near Tetuan] to water and obtain fresh provisions.

Owen says, 'we anchored for a few hours, and then sailed for the West Indies.' He does not describe the hectic departure following a change in the wind, when although cattle for his fleet were actually on the beach, Nelson would not wait to take them on board.

Nelson at length passed Gibraltar, after again being obliged to anchor in Rosia Bay. Here he received important information relative to the destination of the French fleet, from Rear-Admiral Campbell, an officer in the Portuguese service. Sadly Campbell was to pay dearly for his loyalty. Dismissed from the Portuguese service, he died in poverty.

Nelson then stood into Lagos Bay, and remained there a few hours while his fleet took on five months' provisions. From this latter place Lord Nelson with his fleet of ten sail of the line, departed for Barbadoes, in pursuit of a force which he knew to be superior to his own by six sail, - a Spanish squadron of five sail of the line having joined the French fleet.

The names and captains of Nelson's fleet were as follows: -

Guns		Vice-Admiral Lord Nelson, K.B.
104	*Victory*	Rear-Admiral George Murray.
		Captain T.M. Hardy.
		Rear-Admiral Thomas Louis.
80	*Canopus*	Captain Francis William Austin.
74	*Superb*	Captain Richard Goodwin Keats.
	Spencer	Captain Hon. Robert Stopford.
	Swiftsure	Captain Mark Robinson.
	Belleisle	Captain William Hargood.
	Conqueror	Captain Israel Pellew.
	Tigre	Captain Bejamin Hallowell.
	Leviathan	Captain Henry William Bayntun.
	Donegal	Captain Pultney Malcolm.

Frigates – *Amazon*, Captain William Parker, *Décade*, Captain W.G. Rutherford; and *Amphion*, Captain Samuel Sutton.

On the 15th May the fleet obtained a sight of the Desertos, and a fine favourable breeze carried the ships joyfully along until, on the 4th June, they arrived in Carlisle Bay, Barbadoes. At this place Lord Nelson expected to be joined by six sail of the line, but found only the *Northumberland* and *Spartiate*. Here the *Belleisle* and other ships took on board troops (one wing of the 6th India Regiment on the *Belleisle*) as it was considered probable that the French intended to make an attack upon Trinidad; and for that place, accordingly, the fleet departed on the following day, reinforced by the two ships before named.

Trinidad was reached on the 7th June, but the fleet was unable to pass the Boca until the next morning, when fully expecting to find the French fleet in the Gulf of Paria.

Nelson pushed for that place, and anchored there at five p.m. His disappointment at finding himself again defrauded of his prey was great, as might be supposed; but he did not want for fellow sufferers in the persons of his captains, none of whom, probably felt more on the occasion than Hargood.

Nelson's frustration at his dependence on the wind emerges in the following letter.

Victory, July 1st, 1805.

My dear Hargood,

As the day is very fine, I was in hopes that you would have come on board and dined. From winds, and the expectation of wind, I have been afraid to ask my friends to dinner; but I need not, I hope, assure you, how glad I am always to see you, being my dear Hargood,

Yours most faithfully,
Nelson & Brontë.

Finding M. Villeneuve had left the West Indies, the fleet returned homeward after disembarking the troops, and on the 9th July obtained sight of St Michael's and arrived at Gibraltar on the 19th.

11

'I WILL GIVE THEM SUCH A SHAKING'

From Gibraltar the *Belleisle* with the fleet again weighed on the 24th, and, still searching for the French fleet, joined the Channel fleet off Ushant, under Sir William Cornwallis, on the 16th August.

Sir William Cornwallis was the man who taught Nelson the maxim: 'You can always beat a Frenchman if you fight him long enough'. Appointed Commander-in Chief of the Channel fleet by Lord St. Vincent in 1801 (when the latter became First Lord of the Admiralty) he took over ships renowned for the efficiency of their crews. Nonetheless, it was his strategy which defeated Napoleon's plan to invade Britain in the summer of 1805.

The French Admiral Pierre, Comte de Villeneuve (one of the few officers of the French aristocracy who had survived the Revolution) had achieved what Napoleon wanted by leading Nelson on a wild goose chase to the West Indies. Once there, however, he had failed to join up with the fleet commanded by Ganteaume, because it was still blockaded by Cornwallis in Brest. Thus, when the time limit ended, Villeneuve took his fleet back to Europe.

Nelson, again in pursuit, thought he was heading for Cadiz. He dispatched HMS *Curieux*, a fast-sailing brig, to tell the Admiralty that he was on their tail. The ship made such speed, however, that she overtook the French fleet in mid-ocean and her captain, Captain Bettesworth, guessed correctly that they were in fact heading for Spain.

Nelson was furious that Bettesworth had not returned to bring him the news. However, Bettesworth, faced with the dilemma of

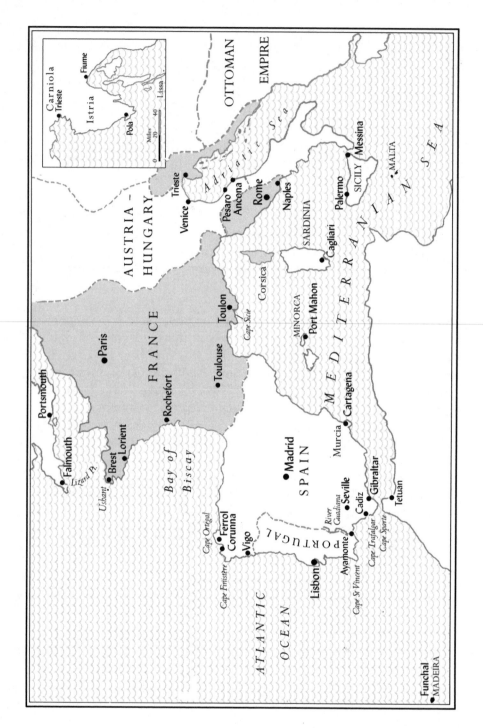

Carniola
Trieste
Fiume
Istria
Pola
Miles
20 40
Lissa

OTTOMAN
EMPIRE

Messina
SICILY
MALTA
Palermo
Naples

Adriatic Sea

Venice
Trieste

AUSTRIA –
HUNGARY

Pesaro
Ancona
Rome

SARDINIA
Cagliari

MEDITERRANEAN SEA

Corsica
Cape Sicie
Toulon

MINORCA
Port Mahon

Paris
FRANCE
Toulouse

Portsmouth

Rochefort

Falmouth
Lorient
Lizard Pt.
Brest
Ushant

Bay of
Biscay

Madrid
SPAIN
Murcia
Cartagena

Gibraltar
Seville
Cadiz
Tetuan

Cape Ortigal
Ferrol
Corunna
Vigo

River
Guadiana
PORTUGAL

Ayamonte
Cape Trafalgar
Cape Spartel

Cape Finisterre

Lisbon

Cape St Vincent

ATLANTIC
OCEAN

Funchal
MADEIRA

92

which way he should go, made the right decision as it later transpired. Piling on all sail he headed for the English Channel and told Vice-Admiral Cornwallis what he had seen. Cornwallis then immediately ordered Admiral Calder to sail with a squadron to intercept the returning French fleet.

Calder found Villeneuve off Cape Finisterre where a battle was fought on 22 July. Unfortunately for Calder, a thick mist came down so that most of the French ships slipped past him and made it to safety in the nearby almost land-locked harbour of Vigo.

Nelson reached Cadiz to find no sign of the French fleet. Bitterly disappointed, he poured out his frustration to his old friend Hargood in a letter dated 5 August. Presumably owing to slowness of communications, he had not yet heard of Calder's battle a fortnight before. Alternately, if he had done so, he was fuming at not having been at the scene of action when he would, undoubtedly, have allowed few if any of the enemy to escape.

There must have been some sort of trouble in the *Belleisle*, presumably from one of the crew, to which Nelson refers:

Victory, August 5th, 1805.
   My dear Hargood,
   Nothing but your desire to save the . . . of the Belleisle from the fate which would justly await him, should your charges against him be proved, could have induced me to allow of your forgiveness of such faults as his have been; and I sincerely hope that he will show his gratitude to you for this great proof of your goodness to him. I hope you will severely admonish him, and that his future conduct will show his sincere contrition.
                    I am ever, dear Hargood,
                     Yours most faithfully,
                      Nelson & Brontë.

I am dreadfully uneasy at not getting a fair wind; - I feel every moment an age, for the enemy's fleet may be off Ireland or in the Channel. You were told by telegraph that the *Curieux* saw the combined squadron on June 19th; I am sorry that Captain Bettesworth did not stand back and try to find us out. I feel very unlucky. I need not say I shall always be glad to see you.

Nelson, in a state of despondency over what he felt sure was a missed opportunity to achieve a decisive victory, decided to return to England for leave which was greatly overdue. Having left Collingwood with three ships to guard the harbour of Cadiz, he joined his fleet to that commanded by Cornwallis. The combined fleet, Calder having rejoined, now numbered thirty-eight ships.

Lieutenant Owen writes:

'On the 19th July we again anchored at Gibraltar, and on the 15th August joined the Channel fleet off Brest, commanded by Admiral Cornwallis. This junction has been described by persons in Cornwallis's fleet as having been one of the most beautiful naval operations ever seen; Nelson's squadron having been all freshly painted in an uniform manner, in a high state of discipline and in trim order. The Belleisle was dispatched the same night to Plymouth, and there docked and refitted.'

Napoleon had now succeeded in causing the very last thing he wanted, a powerful group of ships guarding the Channel.

A week after this, on 22 August, Napoleon sent a messenger to Villeneuve who, unknown to him, had just reached Cadiz, ordering him to 'lose not a moment but enter the Channel with my united fleets. England is ours; we are quite ready and everything is embarked. Come only for twenty-four hours and all is over.'

Amazingly, on the next day Napoleon changed his mind. Throwing his plans for invading Britain to the winds, he wheeled his troops about and marched them instead into Austria, where on 2 December he was to win the battle of Austerlitz which virtually made him the master of Europe.

Meanwhile, in the last week of August, Villeneuve had obeyed his orders. Nelson had only just departed for England when word had reached Cornwallis that the French Admiral had left Vigo and put to sea. Immediately he had sent Calder south again with a squadron of twenty ships. Somehow, Villeneuve had got wind of it and, knowing that his poorly trained crew could not contend with the strong enemy force which was bearing down to attack him, had promptly sailed south for Cadiz.

Napoleon, when told of this happening, flew into a passionate rage. 'What a fleet! What sacrifices for nothing! What an admiral! All hope is gone!'[1] Accusing Villeneuve of treachery and cowardice, he promptly relieved him of his command, appointing Admiral Rosily in his place.

Villeneuve, informed of what was happening, waited for a chance to leave Cadiz. A successful action against the British was the only way to clear his name. Already he had been informed that Rosily was on his way.

As all this was taking place the ships of the British Channel Fleet continued to act as watchdogs, sailing up and down the French coast. The *Belleisle*, however, being much in need of repair, was ordered to part company and proceed to Plymouth, where she arrived early in September and anchored in Cawsand Bay.

On his arrival at Plymouth Captain Hargood wrote to his old friend the Duke of Clarence, acquainting him with his cruise, and received the following letter in return:

Bushy House,
Thursday night [September 1805].

Dear Hargood,

I am to acknowledge yours of the 27th August, from Plymouth, and applaud your zeal in remaining at the present moment with the ship. Lord Nelson I have seen, and he speaks of you in those favourable terms that I am convinced you merit, and which give me great satisfaction. I am glad to find Lieutenant Pascoe is well thought of by his Lordship.

That man must be an enemy to his king and country that does not regret the fleet under Lord Nelson did not fall in with the enemy. However, our victory is only delayed; and I hope not many months will pass before you will receive the medal for some decisive action.

I trust young Redwood and the two Kings deserve your countenance.[2] As circumstances arise pray write; and ever believe me, whether present or absent,

Yours sincerely
William.

In going into Hamoaze the *Belleisle* grounded on the Asia shoal, but soon got off; and such was the expedition used in order to enable the ship to rejoin the fleet, that in the course of three days she was completely stripped, cleared and hauled into dock. Not having many defects under water, she was undocked the next day, and hauled alongside the sheer hulk to get her mizenmast out, it being sprung. Some little delay occurred on this account, notwithstanding which the ship was got ready for sea with great dispatch, and on the 23rd September worked out of Hamoaze to Cawsand Bay, with the wind at north and north north-east.

This was a tremendous feat of seamanship before the days of steam. Years later, when Hargood, by then, Admiral Sir William, was Commander-in-Chief at Plymouth, a lieutenant, ordered to take a small brig into the Sound when there was little wind, had the temerity to ask for a steamship to tow out his brig. Sir William told him sharply that when in command of the *Belleisle* had he not worked out of Hamoaze with the wind two points more against him, he should not have been at Trafalgar. Thus he had better find his way to the Sound without delay!

Captain Hargood sailed from Cawsand Bay on 28 September. His crew included a boy of fifteen, Midshipman Henry Parker, acting as his A.D.C.

On 10 October the *Belleisle* rejoined Lord Nelson off Cadiz, where she continued to cruise, waiting for the combined fleets of France and Spain to put to sea. The port of Cadiz where the masts of the French fleet were crowded as 'thick as a wood' was closely watched by frigates, sailing close to the shore. Meanwhile, just over the horizon, Nelson thirsted for news.

At the same time Admiral Villeneuve, ordered by Napoleon to sail to Naples to support his war against Austria, was waiting for a chance to leave Cadiz. Nearly two weeks had passed since, together with his own and the Spanish admirals, he had held a council of war on board his flagship the *Bucentaure*. Villeneuve had then passed on the Emperor's instructions that the Combined Fleet should weigh at the first opportunity and that 'wherever the enemy should be encountered in inferior strength they must be attacked without hesitation in order to force them to a decisive action'. He had then explained that information had reached him that the British fleet numbered at least thirty-three battleships and asked for their opinions on how to proceed.

The Spanish Chief-of-Staff, Rear-Admiral Escaño, acting as the spokesman for his subordinates, demanded of the French 'whether in the circumstances – the English having twenty-five to thirty ships at the harbour mouth – it were preferable to leave port or to receive an attack at anchor'.

Admiral Escaño then made several acid comments on 'the difference between the skilled seamanship of those [British] who had been at sea with their squadrons without the least intermission since 1793 and those who had spent eight years without putting to sea. He assured the Spanish that they were not able to rely on their short-handed unskilled seamen.' Bluntly he stated that 'Superior orders cannot bind us to attempt the impossible, as nothing could serve as an excuse in the event of a disaster, which I see to be inevitable if we weigh.'

Chaos then reigned within the cabin. The French Rear-Admiral Magon leapt up in a fury to defy Escaño. The Spaniards reacted with equal ferocity. All shouted at each other until eventually the Spanish Commander-in-Chief, Admiral Don Frederico Gravina, calmed them down by suggesting they should take a vote. Should or should not the Combined Fleet, in view that it did not have the superiority in numbers over the British, put to sea?

The majority of both the French and Spanish officers decreed that they should stay at anchor – the decision had been made.

Immediately Villeneuve sent an officer to Paris, carrying the decision of the Council of War to Admiral Decrès, the Minister of Marine. Riding day and night, eating snatched meals in the saddle, the man stopped only to change horses as he galloped north to France through Spain.

On the same day that the Council of War of the Combined Forces took place Nelson sat down in his cabin on the *Victory* to write his Secret Memorandum to his captains, which became famous as the 'Nelson Touch'.

In it he laid out his plans. The Order of Sailing was to be the Order of Battle. There would be two parallel columns. He himself would lead one, Collingwood, his second in command, the other. Collingwood's division would break through the enemy's line about the twelfth ship from the rear, while his own would fall upon and destroy the centre. In this way the whole of the British Fleet (including an advanced squadron of eight ships) would be concentrated on about half of the Combined Fleet. His plan was to defeat them before the remaining ships of the enemy could re-form to take an active part in the battle.

He added, however, that 'something must be left to chance. Nothing is sure in a sea fight beyond all others. Shot will carry away the masts and yards of friends as well as foes; but I look with

SEE PAGE 38

confidence to a victory before the van of the enemy could succour their friends.'

The strategy was both bold and original. It was also exceptionally dangerous, particularly for the leading ships of both lines, which, by approaching the French ships head on, must for some time be exposed to their broadsides while unable to fire in return.

Nelson's plan, elaborated in greater detail, with jerky movements of his left hand, was transcribed in a more readable version by his secretary, John Scott, who sent copies to each of the captains the next day. Included was Captain James Morris, newly arrived on the *Colossus*, on 29 September, the day the distribution took place.

Another letter went to Captain Blackwood of the *Euryalus*, who was keeping watch on the enemy at the mouth of the harbour of Cadiz.

> To Captain the Hon. Henry Blackwood,
> HM Ship *Euryalus*
> Victory, October 10th, 1805, Cadiz, East, 13 Leagues.
> My dear Blackwood,
>
> Keep your five frigates, *Weazle* and *Pickle,* and let me know every movement. I rely on you that we can't miss getting hold of them, and I will give them such a shaking as they never experienced: at least I will lay down my life in the attempt. We are a very powerful fleet and not to be held cheap.
>
> I have told Parker, and do you direct Ships, bringing information of their coming out, to fire guns every three minutes by the watch, and in the night to fire off rockets, if they have them, from the mast-head.
>
> I have nothing more to say, than I hope they will sail tonight
> Ever yours most faithfully,
> Nelson and Brontë.

On the day that this letter was written, Thursday, 10 October, the *Belleisle*, commanded by Captain Hargood, arrived to join Nelson's fleet.

Meanwhile, lying close in to Cadiz, Captain Henry Blackwood kept watch on the enemy fleet. His ship the *Euryalus* was the first of a near invisible chain over which news could be flashed to Nelson by means of lights and flags. Next, just within sight, was the 74-gun *Defence* (Captain George Hope). Farther again, on the horizon lay the *Agamemnon,* her Captain, Edward Berry, being one of Nelson's special friends. Beyond him again was the *Colossus*, her Captain James Morris being he who had lost his father on the *Bristol*. The last link was the *Mars*, commanded by the handsome George Duff from the Scottish town of Banff.

Nine days passed without action as the British ships wore and tacked. Then, on Saturday, 19 October, Villeneuve, knowing that Admiral Rosily was already on his way to replace him, decided to chance his fate. He had made up his mind to challenge Nelson. If he failed and lost his life in doing so he would at least die with honour. The alternative, as he knew only too well, was a court martial, precluding total disgrace.

Saturday, 19 October dawned fair. The British fleet was sailing in two divisions, the one to windward led by Nelson, the other to leeward by Collingwood. Nelson wrote to Collingwood, asking him to dinner. 'What a beautiful day! Will you be tempted out of your ship? If you will, hoist the "assent" and Victory's pendants'. He then sent a midshipman in one of the *Victory*'s boats to deliver the letter to the *Royal Sovereign*.

Collingwood, having read it, was just about to reply when a diversion occurred which put everything else from his mind. The first lieutenant of the *Bellerophon,* [Captain John Cooke] the fourth ship in Collingwood's division, a sharp-eyed young man called William Cumby, noticed a hoist of flags flying from the masthead of the *Mars*. Through his telescope he looked again, hardly believing that he was seeing the signal for which they had all waited for so long – a yellow diagonal cross on a blue background, blue, white and blue vertical stripes, and a flag divided diagonally in white and blue, No. 370 in the Signal Book for Ships of War: *The enemy's ships are coming out of port, or are getting under sail.* Cumby looked again. Yes, they were still there. He rushed to tell Captain Cooke, but neither he nor any of the other officers and signalmen could see well enough to identify signal 370.

'The *Mars* at that time was so far from us', wrote Cumby, 'that her topgallant-masts alone were visible above the horizon, and consequently the distance was so great for the discovery of the *colours* of the flags that Captain Cooke said he was unwilling to repeat a signal of so much importance unless he could clearly distinguish the flags himself, which on looking through his glass he declared he was unable to do . . . Soon afterwards the *Mars* hauled the flags down, and I said, "Now she will make the distant signal 370." [Distant signals were used in cases when it was difficult to see colours distinctly. Those for 370 were a flag, a ball and a pendant.] Sure enough she did make the distant signal, as I had predicted; this could not be mistaken and we were preparing to repeat it, the *Mars*'s signal was answered from the *Victory,* and immediately afterwards the dinner signal was annulled and the signal given for a general chase.'[3]

'It was on the 19th, at 9.30 am,' writes Mr James, 'whilst the British fleet was lying-to about sixteen leagues west-south-west from Cadiz, that the *Mars,* who with the *Defence* and *Agamemnon* then formed the cordon of communication between the *Euryalus* and *Victory,* repeated the signal (370) that the enemy were coming out of port. Lord Nelson immediately made sail in chase to the south-east, with light and partial breezes mostly from the south-west. At 3 pm the *Colossus* [Captain Morris] repeated the signal that the enemy was at sea. Towards evening Lord Nelson directed that the fleet should observe the motions of the *Victory* during the night; that the *Britannia, Dreadnought,* and *Prince,* being heavy sailers, should take their stations as most convenient to them; and that the *Mars, Orion, Belleisle, Leviathan, Bellerophon* and *Polyphemus* should proceed ahead, carry a light, and steer for the strait's mouth.'

> Nothing, however, was seen of the combined fleets that night, and on the morning of the 20th the British lookout ships were near the rock of Gibraltar, but out of sight of the enemy. The British fleet then wore, and made sail to the north-west, with a fresh breeze at south south-west.
>
> Towards the evening of this day the British look-out frigates again obtained a sight of the combined fleets, and Captain Blackwood in the Euryalus was entrusted to keep sight of them and watch their motions during the night

'On Sunday, the 20th, it appears to have been ascertained that the intention of the enemy was to pass the Streights [sic]and enter the Mediterranean.' writes Owen. He adds that 'at this time the fore-sight of Lord Nelson was evinced by what unpractised persons would have called a trifle, but which was in reality a circumstance of great importance to the *Belleisle,* which happened to be the only ship of the fleet which had the hoops of her lower masts painted black, while it was universally done in the French ships. The Admiral therefore, by signal, directed the *Belleisle* to paint the hoops of her masts yellow, because in action the masts would be seen through the smoke when the hull could not, and the *Belleisle* would thereby become liable to be fired into by the British ships.

'For a similar reason, although the Admiral's flag was red, the fleet was ordered to fight under the St George's or white ensign, to mark their colours more distinctly from those of the French in the smoke, the fly of the French ensign being red. At sunset on this day the lookout squadron took their places in the order of sailing in the fleet; and the Admiral telegraphed to Captain Blackwood, "I depend upon your keeping sight of the enemy during the night."'

On the morning of the 21st the British fleet, in consequence of the manoeuvres of Lord Nelson during the night, was only about nine or ten, or some say twelve, miles distant from the enemy's fleet, which was inshore and to leeward, bearing about east. It was then that the action appeared inevitable, and the cheers of the crews of the British ships gave satisfactory proof of their feelings.

12

PLUNDERING THE CAPTAIN'S GRAPES.
THE BATTLE OF TRAFALGAR

First-hand accounts of the battle of Trafalgar are given by First
Lieutenant John Owen, of the Marines and by 2nd Lieutenant Paul
Harris Nicolas, Royal Marines, then aged sixteen, on board the
Belleisle. His story is taken from the magazine *Bijou* of 1829.
Descriptions are also taken from family papers edited by John
Somers Cocks, a descendant of the sisters who married William
Hargood and James Nicoll Morris.

Nicolas begins the tale:

'I was scarcely sixteen when I embarked for the first time, in the
Belleisle of 74 guns, and joined the fleet off Cadiz, under
the command of Lord Nelson, in the early part of October, 1805.

As the day dawned the horizon appeared covered with ships. The
whole force of the enemy was discovered standing to the southward,
distant about nine miles, between us and the coast near Trafalgar. I
was awakened by the cheers of the crew and by their rushing up the
hatchways to get a glimpse of the hostile fleet. The delight manifested exceeded anything I ever witnessed, surpassing even those
gratulations when our native cliffs are descried after a long period
of distant service. There was a light air from the north-west with a
heavy swell. The signal to bear up and make all sail, and to form the
order of sailing in two divisions, was thrown out. The *Victory*, Lord
Nelson's ship, leading the weather line, and the *Royal Sovereign*,
bearing the flag of Admiral Collingwood, the second in command,
the lee line.'

At this time the *Belleisle* was the third ship of the lee line, which
was led in gallant style by Vice-Admiral Collingwood, in the

Royal Sovereign. But the wind was very light, and the *Tonnant*, the ship at that time ahead of the *Belleisle*, sailed so heavily, that although she had all sail set, the *Belleisle* could with difficulty keep her station under her plain sails. At eight the wind falling still lighter, the *Royal Sovereign* [which had been newly coppered]was increasing her distance from the *Tonnant*, and consequently from the *Belleilse* and the ships of the division. The combined fleets were at this time plainly to be seen, and under easy sail on the starboard tack.

Nicolas describes how 'The officers now met at breakfast; and though each seemed to exult in the hope of a glorious termination to the contest so near at hand, a fearful presage was experienced that all would not again unite at that festive board. One was particularly impressed with a persuasion that he should not survive the day, nor could he divest himself of this presentiment, but made the necessary disposal of his property in the event of his death. The sound of the drum, however, soon put an end to our meditations and after a hasty and, alas! a final farewell to some, we repaired to our respective posts.'

At twenty minutes past nine the *Royal Sovereign*, made the *Belleisle* and *Tonnant* signals to change places in the line, and for the *Belleisle* to make more sail. Never was a signal more welcome; and in the course of a few minutes the *Belleisle*, with her royals set, and studdingsails booming out on both sides, was passing the *Tonnant* in obedience to Vice-Admiral Collingwood's signal.

'On our passing that ship,' writes Nicolas, ' the captains greeted each other on the honourable prospect in view: Captain Tyler [*Tonnant*] exclaimed, "A glorious day for old England! We shall have one apiece before night!" This confidence in our professional superiority – which carries such terror to other nations – seemed expressed in every countenance; and as if in confirmation of this soul-inspiring sentiment, the band of our consort was playing "Britons strike home".'

The band on a warship usually consisted of some of the crew who thumped away with much enthusiasm if not with great expertise.

At half-past nine the *Belleisle*, then fast closing with the *Royal Sovereign*, was ordered to bear south-west, and in ten minutes afterwards to alter course one point to starboard. It was about this time – and which probably gave rise to this change of course – that the combined fleets were hove-to on the larboard tack, and hoisted their colours. With the wind so light as it was, the patience of English sailors was put to a severe test, as the ships, notwithstanding every inch of canvas which could be spread was set, could not go ahead at a greater rate than about two miles an hour: but they were yet to endure a more severe trial before they could have an opportunity of using their guns.

While the leading ships of the lee division were going into action, Nelson was confusing the enemy's van. Only when Rear-Admiral Dumanoir's squadron had been drawn well away to the north did he suddenly alter course and steer straight for the centre of their fleet. Choosing the largest ships as his target he was soon in the fight, closely supported by the *Temeraire* and the other ships of the weather division. One after another they bore down and cut through the line and engaged the enemy.

The Combined Fleet presented a frightening but colourful sight. The sun, which had now broken through the mist, shone down on the line of yellow, black, red and white, sailing slowly and majestically through a deep blue sea. A group of particularly large ships lay near their centre: Rear-Admiral Cisneros's huge *Santissima Trinidad*, the largest vessel in the world, painted a vivid vermilion and white with a prominent white figurehead; the French flagship *Bucentaure* carrying Admiral Villeneuve; the grim black hull of Admiral de Alava's *Santa Ana*, and other elaborately decorated Spanish ships, 'A bunch of beauties' as one sailor called them, which all agreed would make a brave sight as prizes at Spithead.

In contrast to the men in the Combined Fleet, the English ships, painted ochre and black under their snowy white canvas, looked forbidding. The French sailors afterwards admitted their fear as the two lines advanced slowly but inexorably down upon them, gently rising and falling on the oily swell, completely unflinching even after heavy fire had been opened on them.

Collingwood was steering for the *Santa Ana*, the sixteenth ship from the rear end of the enemy's line. A four-decker carrying 112 guns, her black hull towering above the sea, he knew her to be the flagship of the Spanish Vice-Admiral de Alava. Behind him, in the *Belleisle*, Hargood also recognized the flag of his old adversary de Alava, he whom he had vanquished in the Straits of Malacca while in command of the *Intrepid*, in February 1799. Now, in the space of minutes, they would fight again.

At eleven Vice-Admiral Collingwood made the signal for the *Belleisle* to close the *Royal Sovereign*, which every effort was, and always had been, made to do; and it will be seen that the *Royal Sovereign* did not long want a second in the action. At about twenty minutes before twelve Lord Nelson threw out his never-to-be-forgotten signal:
'England expects every man to do his duty.'

Sir Home Popham's 'dictionary' for the Royal Navy had been issued in 1800. Consisting of nearly a thousand words, it numbered up to 999. A second addition containing another thousand words had appeared in 1803 and, finally, a third, with nearly a thousand 'sentences most applicable to military or general conversation' had come out. A ball or a pendant above the three flags of the hoist indicated the second book. The same below meant the third.

Nelson's immortal signal was sent in this last-named code. He meant to hoist 'England **confides** etc,' but his flag lieutenant, John Pasco, pointed out that this would have to be spelt out in full, whereas '**expects**' could be made in one hoist. Nelson therefore agreed to the change. Only the last word '**duty**' was actually made in four hoists. Nicolas remembered how 'As this emphatic injunction was communicated through the decks, it was received with enthusiastic cheers, and each bosom glowed with ardour at this appeal to individual valour.'

A few minutes afterwards the enemy commenced firing upon the two leading ships of the lee line. The *Fougueux*, French 74, was the first ship to fire, followed by the *Santa Ana*, Spanish 110 [bearing the flag of Admiral Hargood's old enemy, Stet Vice-Admiral don Ignacio de Alava] and several other ships, and a severe cross fire was kept up, which especially to the *Belleisle*, was productive of much loss.
[Broadly speaking the French gunners fired chiefly at their enemy's rigging while the English concentrated on the hulls.]

'Although until that moment we had not fired a shot,' writes Nicolas, 'Our sails and rigging bore evident proofs of the manner in which we had been treated: our mizen top mast was shot away and the ensign had been thrice rehoisted; numbers lay dead upon the decks, and eleven wounded were already in the surgeon's care.'

[Midshipman Henry Parker, Hargood's ADC, was badly wounded in the throat later in the battle as he struggled to attach a union jack to the stump of one of the masts of the *Belleisle*]

Nicolas continues, 'The firing was now tremendous; and at intervals the dispersion of the smoke gave us a sight of the colours of our adversaries.' Owen takes up the story. 'At half-past eleven, as we were slowly approaching the enemy, they hoisted their colours, which showed us that the French and Spanish ships were chequered in their line, which was curved, the van and rear being more to windward than the centre.

'At a quarter before twelve seven or eight of the enemy's ships opened their fire upon the *Royal Sovereign* and the *Belleisle*; and as we were steering directly for them we could only remain passive, and perversely approach the position we were to occupy in this great battle.

'This was a trying moment. Captain Hargood had taken his station at the forepart of the quarterdeck on the starboard side, occasionally standing on a carronade slide, whence he issued his orders for the men to lie down at their quarters, and with the utmost coolness directed the steering of the ship. The silence on board was almost awful, broken only by the firm voice of the Captain, 'steady' or 'starboard a little!' which was repeated by the master to the quartermaster at the helm; and occasionally by an officer calling to the now impatient men, Lie down there, you sir!'

'As we got nearer and nearer to the enemy the silence was, however, broken frequently by the sadly stirring shrieks of the wounded, for of them, and killed, we had more than fifty before we fired a shot.'

Owen continues: 'Seeing that our men were falling fast, the first lieutenant ventured to ask Captain Hargood if he had not better show his broadside to the enemy and fire, if only to cover the ship with smoke? The gallant man's reply was somewhat stern but emphatic:- "No, we are ordered to go through the line, and go through she shall by . . . .".'

*   *   *

Discipline was clearly superb, and Hargood, immaculate in a frock coat with gold epaulettes, silk breeches and stockings and buckled shoes, set a fine example by pacing his quarter-deck as though nothing was happening at all.

Nicolas, the scene still vivid in his mind, gives his own description of what Owen has just described: 'About half-past eleven the *Royal Sovereign* fired three guns, which had the intended effect of inducing the enemy to hoist their colours, and showed us the tricoloured flag intermixed with that of Spain.'

'At noon,' according to an entry in the *Belleisle*'s journal, 'that ship was distant from the enemy's line near three-quarters of a mile, and only two cable-lengths astern of the *Royal Sovereign*, there being then a light air of wind with a long ground swell.'

According to her rate of sailing, however, she could not have been at so great a distance from the enemy, for other notes immediately follow.

At five minutes past noon the *Royal Sovereign* cut the enemy's line astern of a Spanish three-decker . . . at eight minutes past opened fire on the enemy . . . and at thirteen minutes past cut enemy's line astern of a French 80-gun ship, second to the Spanish Vice-Admiral' [the *Santa Ana*].

The *Belleisle*, therefore, at noon could not have been above a quarter of a mile distant, and at this time, although a most severe, well directed and destructive fire had been kept up for upwards of a quarter of an hour, Captain Hargood would not permit a single shot to be fired in return, but, with every stitch of canvas set, pushed forward to support his gallant leader.

Nicolas continues. 'The drum now repeated the summons, and the Captain sent for the officers commanding at their various quarters. "Gentlemen," said he, "I have only to say that I shall pass close under the stern of that ship; put in two round shot and then a grape, and give her *that*. Now go to your quarters and mind not to fire until each gun will bear with effect." With this laconic instruction the gallant little man posted himself on the slide of the foremost carronade on the starboard side of the quarterdeck.' [Being so short of stature he actually climbed onto the gun carriage, the better to see the enemy ships ahead, already half-covered by their smoke.]

'The determined and resolute countenance of the weather-beaten sailor, here and there brightened by a smile of exultation, was well suited to the terrific appearance which they exhibited. Some were stripped to the waist; some had bared their necks and arms; others had tied a handkerchief round their heads; and all seemed eagerly to await the order to engage. My two brother officers and myself were stationed, with about thirty men at small arms, on the poop, on the front of which I was now standing. The shot began to pass over us and gave us intimation of what we should in a few minutes undergo. An awful silence prevailed in the ship only interrupted by the commanding voice of Captain Hargood, "Steady! starboard a little! Steady so!" echoed by the master directing the quartermasters at the wheel.

'A shriek soon followed, – a cry of agony was produced by the next shot– and the loss of the head of a poor recruit was the effect of the succeeding, – and, as we advanced, destruction rapidly increased. A severe contusion in the breast now prostrated our Captain, but he soon resumed his station. Those only who have been in a similar situation to the one I am attempting to describe, can have a correct idea of such a scene. My eyes were horror-struck at the bloody corpses around me, and my ears rang with the shrieks of the wounded and the moans of the dying.

'At this moment, seeing that almost everyone was lying down, I was half disposed to follow the example, and several times stooped for the purpose; but – and I remember the impression well – a certain monitor seemed to whisper "stand up and do not shrink from your duty!" Turning round my much esteemed and gallant senior (Lieutenant John Owen) fixed my attention; the serenity of his countenance and the composure with which he paced the deck drove more than half my terrors away; and joining him I became somewhat infused with his spirit, which cheered me on to act the part it became me. My experience is an instance of how much depends on the example of those in command when exposed to the fire of the enemy, more particularly in the trying situation in which we were placed for nearly thirty minutes, from not having the power to retaliate'. [The waiting was becoming intolerable: almost more than most on board the *Belleisle* could bear.]

'This state of things,' wrote Owen, 'had lasted about twenty minutes, and it required the tact of the more experienced officers to keep up the spirits of those around them, by observing that "We

108

should soon begin our work". Our energies were joyfully called into play by "Stand to your guns!"'

At about fifteen minutes after noon the *Belleisle* followed the *Royal Sovereign* through the French line. Then came a thunderous roar as her gunners discharged both broadsides practically simultaneously. The *Santa Ana* and the *Fougueux* which lay to starboard, were both raked with a terrible fire. But a second French ship, the *Indomptable*, was nearly doubling the *Santa Ana* in the line.

Nicolas takes up the story.

'At this critical period, while steering for the stern of the *Indomptable* (our masts and yards and sails hanging in utmost confusion over our heads) which continued a most galling raking fire upon us, the *Fougueux* being on our starboard quarter, and the Spanish *San Justo* on our larboard bow, the Master earnestly addressed the Captain to know what he should do next. `Shall we go through, Sir?'

'"Go through by–!" was his energetic reply. "There's your ship sir [pointing to the *Indomptable*] place me close alongside of her.' [However] our opponent defeated this manoeuvre by bearing away in a parallel course.'

Captain Sir George Westphal, then a midshipman on the *Victory*, wrote, 'I had left my quarters to make a report to Quilliam, our first lieutenant, who was standing near Lord Nelson on the quarter-deck, watching the *Belleisle*, who every person thought would have opened her fire long before she did, the enemy having been firing at her, and, indeed, having *visibly* damaged her spars some time previously; but the *Belleisle* still reserved her fire until she had brought both broadsides, as appeared to us in the *Victory*, to bear upon ships on each side of her, and was within pistol shot, when her two broadsides were discharged spontaneously, and with the precision of a volley of musketry; upon seeing which Lord Nelson exclaimed, "Nobly done Hargood!"'

By this time the *Belleisle* and the *Indomptable* were fighting it out, broadside to broadside at very close range. They were wrecking each other in a marathon struggle when the *Fougueux*, closing on the starboard side of the *Belleisle*, struck her amidships.

In the next few minutes of desperate fighting, with the two ships locked together, the *Belleisle* lost her maintopmast and her mizzenmast. Not only was she thus made almost unmanageable but the wreckage trailing over her side masked many of her guns. Then, as

109

Belleisle's track

Santa Ana

R. Sov.

the French *Achille* began firing from astern, the *Belleisle* was engaging three ships, while her crew tried frantically to manoeuvre her by putting oars out of the gun-room ports and rowing her round.

Nicolas, the impressions still vivid after over twenty years, wrote, 'The firing was now tremendous; and at intervals the dispersion of the smoke gave us a sight of the colours of our adversaries.

'About one o'clock the *Fougueux* ran us on board on the starboard side; and we continued thus engaging until the latter dropped astern.'

But this gave no respite to the beleaguered ship. The *Indomptable* continued for some time to fire at the *Belleisle* and *Royal Sovereign*. Then she filled, bore up, and left the *Belleisle*, her place being by this time occupied by fresh ships.

> The situation of the *Belleisle* at this time was one of imminent danger, and nothing but the vigour with which her guns were plied, kept her from being surrounded and either sunk or captured.
>
> The cause of the particularly dangerous situation of her at this time, will be more clearly illustrated by the accompanying diagram, showing the positions of the *Belleisle* and the enemy's fleet at about a quarter-past twelve, the time when she commenced the action.
>
> The diagram (see above) shows that at the time the *Belleisle* passed through the enemy's line, fourteen ships of the enemy,

besides the *Fougueux* had to pass her in order to reach the main scene of action. As for the most part they did pass her, or at least got within shot of her, it was not likely they would do so without bestowing upon her a broadside. It will be seen that until relieved by some of her companions, the *Belleisle* had never less than three ships firing upon her at one time.

At forty minutes past twelve the *Belleisle*'s maintopmast was shot away, and at one o'clock she had three ships engaging her at the same time. The ship's journal proceeds. 'At one o'clock a French ship bore up to rake us, and a ship on each side engaging; at ten minutes past the mizenmast was shot way about six feet above the poop.

Between one and two pm the battle was at its height. The action took place towards the centre of the line over a distance of less than two miles. Here the ships thundered at one another beneath a canopy of smoke, muzzle to muzzle. The men dashed buckets of water over smouldering timbers, loaded, fired, and reloaded, while rival boarding parties fought one another off amidst yells, a hail of shot and crashing masts, spars and rigging.

In the midst of this turmoil, at about half past one, Nelson was struck by a bullet fired by a sharpshooter in the rigging of the *Redoutable*.

Some ten minutes before this the *Fougueux*, by now a near total wreck, had sheered off the *Belleisle*. But, almost as Nelson was shot, a fresh ship – the [French] *Achille* – passed under the *Belleisle*'s stern, and subsequently stationed herself on her larboard quarter; and the *Aigle*, after having escaped from the *Bellerophon*, almost immediately afterwards occupied the place of the *Fougueux*.

By this time the *Belleisle*, from her unequal contest, was totally unmanageable, having had all her sails and rigging shot away, and her foremast and mainmast in a tottering state; still, however, the gallant crew opposed an incessant fire from every part of the ship. In this situation she continued – a target for every passing ship – until at ten minutes past two, her mainmast fell aft on the larboard side of the poop.

Nicolas describes his own lucky escape. 'Our mizenmast soon went, and soon afterwards the maintopmast. A two-decked ship, the

[French]*Neptune,* 80, then took a position on our bow, and a 74, the [French] *Achille,* on our quarter. At two o'clock the mainmast fell over the larboard side; I was at the time under the break of the poop, aiding in running out a carronade, when a cry of "Stand clear there! Here it comes!" made me look up, and at that instant the mainmast fell over the bulwarks just above me. This ponderous mass made the whole ship's frame shake, and had it taken a central direction it would have gone through the poop and added many to our list of sufferers.'

At half-past two another comparatively fresh 80-gun ship – the [French] *Neptune* – placed herself on the starboard bow of the *Belleisle,* and shortly afterwards, the ship's foremast fell over the starboard bow, carrying with it the bowsprit and figurehead.

Nicolas, describing this, says, 'At half-past two our foremast was shot away close to the deck. In this unmanageable state we were but seldom capable of annoying our antagonists, while they had the power of choosing their distance, and every shot from them did considerable execution.'

Lieutenant Owen continues: 'Thus was the *Belleisle* a total wreck, without the means of returning the fire of the enemy except from the very few guns still unincumbered by the wreck of the masts and rigging.

Every exertion, however, continued to be made for presenting the best resistance, and offering the greatest annoyance to the enemy; guns were run out from the sternposts on each deck, and all that intelligence could suggest and discipline effect was done. Our loss was, however, becoming severe; the first and junior lieutenants had both been killed on the quarterdeck early in the action; and about the same time the Captain was knocked down and severely injured by a splinter, but refused to leave the deck.

'As we were lying in this dismasted state surrounded by enemy's ships, and not having seen the colours of a friendly ship for the previous two hours, the Captain, seeing me actively employed in my duty, was kind enough to bring me a bunch of grapes, and seemed pleased when I told him that our men were doing nobly, and that the ship had been greatly distinguished.'

[Unknown to Hargood, others had been at his grapes].

Nicolas confesses, 'Some of us had been fortunate in relieving our thirst by plundering the Captain's grapes which hung round his cabin.'

> At three o'clock the *Belleisle*, single-handed, was still engaging the three ships already named and offering as stout a resistance as ever to the overwhelming force opposed to her. But relief was now at hand, and indeed assistance was never more needed.
>
> At twenty minutes past three the *Polyphemus* came down and took off the *Neptune*, and the *Defiance* engaged the *Aigle* at about the same time, but blinded by the smoke of gunfire, the crew of the beleaguered *Belleisle* did not know help was at hand.

'A three decked ship was seen apparently steering towards us', writes Nicolas. 'It can easily be imagined with what anxiety every eye turned towards this formidable object, which would either relieve us from our unwelcome neighbours or render our situation desperate. We had scarcely seen the British colours since one o'clock, and it is impossible to express our emotions as the alteration of the stranger's course displayed the white ensign to our sight.'

Owen takes up the story: 'At half-past three the *Swiftsure*, English 74, came booming through the smoke, passed our stern, and giving us three cheers, placed herself between us and the French ship [the *Achille*] which had been so long more attentive to us than was agreeable. Shortly afterwards the *Polyphemus* took the enemy's ship off our bow, and thus we were at length happily disengaged after nearly four hours struggle, perhaps as severe as ever fell to a British man of war.'

Nicolas says, 'It was near four o'clock when we ceased firing, but the action continued in the body of the fleet about two miles to windward. The van division of the enemy having tacked, it seemed that the fight was about to be renewed. Rear-Admiral Dumanoir, making off with four sail of the line, passed within gun-shot of us; and as we lay in a helpless and solitary situation, our apprehension was much relieved by seeing them proceed silently on their course.'

Dumanoir, by passing to windward, meant to cut off the rearmost ships of Nelson's squadron which had not yet reached the battle. The attempt was a failure. Two of the British ships, the *Minotaur* and

113

the *Spartiate*, attacked and so damaged the French admiral's flag-ship, the *Formidable*, that he decided that to continue the action would only add to the losses of the day.

The battle indeed was over. The British had won largely because of the leadership of their admiral who had inspired all who served under him from the captains down to the ordinary seamen and even the ship's boys, with what he himself called the 'Nelson Touch'.

Another reason was that the gun-crews of the battleships had proved themselves so superior to that of the French. The heavy swell, which had increased in force throughout the day, had made it virtu-ally impossible for the French in their rolling ships, to take accurate aim.

Rear-Admiral Dumanoir was one of the few who escaped. Villeneuve found himself stranded on the *Bucentaure*. The ship herself was virtually wrecked. He, who, by his own words wished to die was one of the few on board who was miraculously left unscathed, but with all her boats shattered by gun-fire he could not transfer his flag to another ship. Therefore, having no alternative, he had ordered his colours to be struck, knowing he must accept the ultimate disgrace. Offering his sword to the Captain of Marines, who had been sent from the *Conqueror* to take possession of his ship, he asked him in English to whom he had the honour of surren-dering. All who saw him as a prisoner were impressed by the dignity with which he subsequently behaved.

Collingwood's own flagship, the *Royal Sovereign*, was now also dismasted and unmanageable after a two-hour battle with the *Santa Ana*. At last, as he saw the Spanish ship haul down her colours, he sent Captain Blackwood to board her. Blackwood, told that Admiral de Alava was dying, returned only with the Captain.

Thus was Captain Hargood deprived of the chance to meet his old antagonist, the Spanish Admiral, who, when in command of the *Intrepid* in 1799, he had chased across the China Seas. Later it tran-spired that Alava, although knocked unconscious, had recovered. Fortune once more had favoured him, so that, as in his former contest with Hargood, he survived to fight again.

The *Tonnant*, in her position behind the *Belleisle* in Collingwood's line collided with the *Algéciras*. As the long bowsprit of the French ship became hooked into the *Tonnant*'s rigging French sailors tried to board her. But even as they did so the British carronades and quarterdeck guns hit them with grape-shot and musket ball and most of them were killed. Nonetheless the battle between the two ships continued for an hour, by the end of which both were dismasted and reduced to hulks.

The *Mars* was similarly damaged during a titanic struggle with the *Fougueux*, during which Captain Duff was killed. With him on board, serving as midshipmen, were his two young sons. The eldest. Lachlan, died in his younger brother's arms.

The *Bellerophon*, bombarded by no less than four French ships, until rescued by the 98-gun *Dreadnought*, was also totally unmanageable. Her captain (Captain Cooke) struck in the chest by two musket-balls, died on the deck.

The *Colossus*, sixth in Collingwood's division, collided with the French *Argonaute* in the blinding smoke from the guns. As the hulls crashed together, driven by the ever-rising swell, cannons simultaneously thundered as the gun-crews fired broadside after broadside into the opposite hulls.

At last those of the *Argonaute* fell silent, and, as the swell lifted her, she drifted away. But Captain Morris, hit by one of her last shots, was badly wounded above the knee. Refusing to be taken down to the surgeon, he wound a tourniquet round his thigh to stop the bleeding and remained in command on the poop. Somehow, although almost fainting from lack of blood, he managed to stay on his feet until, as the tottering mizenmast was about to crash, he consented to limp down to the quarterdeck, just missing being crushed beneath it as it fell.

Next to join in the onslaught on the *Colossus* was the Spanish *Bahama*, which battered her larboard beam. Then hardly had this happened than the French *Swiftsure*, forcing her way between the two ships, received the full force of a broadside from the *Colossus* which blasted her hull to the core. The relentless training of the British gunners was now taking full effect. They fired so quickly and accurately that the *Swiftsure*, badly damaged, drifted astern leaving the *Bahama* to be literally shattered by the guns of the *Colossus*.

Commodore Galiano, on board her, had ordered her colours to be nailed to the mast. 'No Galiano ever surrenders' he declared in the thick of the fight. Wounded, he refused to leave the quarterdeck. The wind from a shot spun the telescope out of his hands and his coxswain, rushing towards him, was cut in two by a cannon ball as he reached his side. Galiano, soaked in his blood, was hit in the head by the next shot and fell dead upon his coxswain's corpse.*

A flag was flung over the Commodore's body to conceal his death from the survivors of his crew. By this time 141 had died out of a total of 690 men on board. The officers who still lived, facing a hopeless situation, held a parley and decided that the nailed-up flag must come down. An English jack was hoisted in its place. Cheers rang out on the *Colossus* when it was realized that the *Bahama* had surrendered to the devastating power of British guns.

Captain Morris, however, had no time to send an officer from the *Colossus* to lay claim to the prize. The French *Swiftsure* was still lurking behind him and Captain Villemadrin saw what he thought to be a chance of slipping in under her stern to put his guns to full use.

But Morris, although now reeling from faintness caused by losing so much blood, foresaw his intentions and gave orders to wear ship. The *Colossus* swung faster than the French ship. Her guns thundered out and the *Swiftsure*'s mizenmast fell. Then down came the maintopmast and the foremast. Captain Villemadrin, knowing his ship to be now virtually immovable, gave orders to cease fire and surrendered.

The *Argonauta*, already so much damaged by the *Colossus*, was finally defeated by the British *Achille*. Allen writes:

'Shortly afterwards the Spanish 80-gun ship, *Argonauta*, which had been engaged by the English *Achille*, and had struck, came down near the *Belleisle* and hoisted English colours. Captain Hargood then directed the master, Mr William Hudson – both the lieutenants on board having been killed – to proceed with a party of hands in the pinnace to take possession of the prize. In this he was accompanied by Lieutenant John Owen of the Marines, who described the carnage which he found.'

13

TEA AT TRAFALGAR.

Nicolas simply states : 'The *Argonauta*, of 80 guns, having surrendered, we sent an officer to take possession; he returned with her
second captain, who stated her loss to amount to two hundred
killed.'

The officer in question was Lieutenant Owen of the marines as
both the lieutenants on deck had been killed.

Owen writes, 'A beaten Spanish 80-gun ship – the *Argonauta* –
having about this time hoisted English colours, the Captain was
good enough to give me the pinnace to take possession of her; the
Master (Mr William Hudson) accompanied me with eight or ten
seamen or marines who happened to be near us. On getting up the
Argonauta's side, I found no living person on her deck, but on my
making my way over numerous dead and a confusion of wreck,
across the quarterdeck, was met by the second captain at the cabin
door, who gave me his sword which I returned, desiring him to keep
it for Captain Hargood to whom I should soon introduce him. With
him I accordingly returned to the *Belleisle,* leaving the Master in
charge of the prize, on board which I had seen only about six officers,
the remainder (amongst whom was the Captain) wounded and all
the men being below out of way of the shot.'

Nicolas spares no detail in describing the carnage on the *Belleisle*:

'Now that the conflict was over our kindlier feelings resumed
their sway. Eager inquiries were expressed, and earnest congratulations exchanged at this joyful moment. The officers came to make
their report to the Captain, and the fatal result cast a gloom over
the scene of our triumph. I have alluded to the impression of our
first lieutenant that he should not survive the contest. This
gallant officer was severely wounded in the thigh, and underwent

amputation: but his prediction was realized, for he expired before the action had ceased. The junior lieutenant was likewise mortally wounded on the quarterdeck. These gallant fellows were lying beside each other in the gunroom preparatory to their being committed to the deep; and here many met to take a last look at their departed friends, whose remains soon followed the promiscuous multitude, without distinction of either rank or nation, to their wide ocean grave. In the act of launching a poor sailor over the poop he was discovered to breathe; he was of course saved, and after being a week in the hospital, the ball which entered the temple came out of his mouth.

'The upper-deck presented a confused and dreadful appearance: masts, yards, sails, ropes, and fragments of wreck, were scattered in every direction; nothing could be more horrible than the scene of blood and mangled remains with which every part was covered, and which, from the quantity of splinters, resembled a shipwright's yard strewed with gore.

'From our extensive loss – thirty-four killed and ninety-six wounded – our cockpit exhibited a scene of suffering and carnage which rarely occurs. I visited this abode of suffering with the natural impulse which led many others thither – namely, to ascertain the fate of a friend or companion. So many bodies in such a confined place and under such distressing circumstances would affect the most obdurate heart. My nerves were but little accustomed to such trials, but even the dangers of the battle did not seem more terrific than the spectacle before me. On a long table lay several anxiously looking for their turn to receive the surgeon's care, yet dreading the fate which he might pronounce. One subject was undergoing amputation, and every part was heaped with sufferers: their piercing shrieks and expiring groans were echoed through this vault of misery; and even at this distant period the heart-sickening picture is alive in my memory. What a contrast to the hilarity and enthusiastic mirth which reigned in this spot the preceding evening!

'At all other times the cockpit is the region of conviviality and good humour, for here it is that the happy midshipmen reside, at whose board neither discord nor care interrupt the social intercourse. But a few short hours since, on these benches, which were now covered with mutilated remains, sat these scions of their country's glory, who hailed the coming hour of conflict with cheerful confidence, and each told his story to beguile the anxious moments; the younger ones eagerly listening to their experienced associates and all united to the toast of "May we meet again as this hour tomorrow!"'

'I have heard some men say that they have not felt anything like fear at the approach of battle. Such stoicism may exist; the nerves of robust constitutions may wholly subdue the weakness of nature: but candour must own that a struggle generally takes place between our sentiments of duty and honour, and that natural feeling which makes us shudder at impending danger. Truly and beautifully has a distinguished writer observed, -

> "The brave man is not he who feels no fear,
>   For that were brutish and irrational;
>   But he whose noble soul its fear subdues,
> And bravely dares the danger nature shrinks from."'

At a quarter past four the *Naiad*, Captain Thomas Dundas, by direction of Captain Hardy, bore down and took the *Belleisle* in tow. At much the same time Lieutenant Owen returned in the pinnace with the captain of the *Argonaute*, Owen describes how:

'Captain Hargood took the Spaniard [Captain Pareja] to his cabin, where he shortly afterwards assembled as many of the officers as could be spared from duty, to the most acceptable refreshment of tea, during which an officer of the *Naiad* frigate – which had in the meantime taken the *Belleisle* in tow – came on board with the news of the death of our heroic Admiral. I well remember the deep sensation which this caused amongst us, and even the Spanish Captain joined in our regret.

'During the time we were enjoying our welcome meal, Captain Hargood observed that my trousers were torn and bloody, and sent for the surgeon, who came reeking from the cockpit, which was crowded with wounded, to examine my hurt, which while the battle lasted I was scarcely conscious of, but after it was over recollected that I had been knocked down early in the action by a splinter, which tore away a small portion of muscle from my left thigh. The surgeon also looked at Captain Hargood's hurt, which was an extensive bruise reaching from the throat nearly to the waist, but he desired not to be returned wounded.'

Nicolas also described that most extraordinary tea party but gives

119

a different version of how those aboard the *Belleisle* heard the news of Nelson's death.

'About five o'clock the officers assembled in the Captain's cabin to take some refreshment. The parching effects of the smoke made this a welcome summons . . . . Four hours' exertion of body, with the energies incessantly employed, occasioned a lassitude, both corporeally and mentally, from which the victorious termination now so near at hand could not arouse us; moreover there sat a melancholy on the brows of some who mourned the messmates who had shared their perils and their vicissitudes for many years. Then the merits of the departed heroes were repeated with a sigh, but their errors sunk with them into the deep. There were few who did not bear some marks of this sanguinary engagement, and those who had the good fortune to escape unhurt presented an appearance which testified the dangers they had encountered.

'Before sunset all firing had ceased. The view of the fleet at this period was highly interesting, and would have formed a beautiful subject for a painter. Just under the setting rays were five or six dismantled prizes; on one hand lay the *Victory* with part of our fleet and prizes, and on the left hand the *Sovereign* and a similar cluster of ships.

'The remnant of the combined fleet was making for Cadiz to the northward; the *Achille* had burnt to the water's edge, with the tricoloured ensign still displayed about a mile from us, and our tenders and boats were using every effect to save the brave fellows who had so gloriously defended her; but only two hundred and fifty were rescued, and she blew up with a tremendous explosion.'

The French *Achille* had been set on fire by a spark from the musket of one of the marksmen stationed in her tops. Her crew, seeing flames spread above them, hacked frantically at the mast, hoping it would fall clear. Burning, she left the battle and stood down wind, but the *Prince,* pursuing her, fired two broadsides, the second of which brought down all three of her masts at once. The mizzen top fell on the boats and the mainmast destroyed the fire pump. Flaming wreckage then fell down to the lower decks. Within minutes the fire was out of control. All who could move scrambled up to the top deck, dragging or carrying as many of the wounded as they could, although many were left in the orlop to die. Hundreds jumped into the sea.

Those on the attacking ships watched in horror as, enemy

though she was, it became obvious that once the fire reached the magazine she would explode. Ceasing their fire, they moved to safe positions, but the crews risked their own lives by rescuing the French sailors in the ship's boats.

Among them was a woman called Jeanette (wife of one of the sailors), who had stowed away on board. Rescued from the sea by one of the *Pickle*'s boats, she was taken on board and given material and needles and thread with which to make herself clothes while an officer lent her his cabin. Captain Moorsom gave her two purser's shirts to make a petticoat and the chaplain pitched in with a pair of shoes. She cried for the loss of her husband but all ended happily in four days time when he was found alive and well.[1]

Also swimming strongly was a large black pig. Rescued, it was taken on board one of the ships and ended up as dinner for the crew.[2]

The Achille never struck her colours. They were flying as Nicolas says, when she finally sank, a vivid ball of flame, into the darkening sea.

Nicolas continues his narrative by describing, differently from Owen, how the news of the death of Nelson reached the *Belleisle*:

'A boat with the lieutenant of the *Entreprenante* shortly after came on board, on his return from the *Victory*, to announce the death of the immortal Nelson. The melancholy tidings spread through the ship in an instant, and its paralysing effect was wonderful. Our Captain had served under the illustrious chief for years, and had partaken in the anxious pursuit of the enemy across the Atlantic with the same officers and crew. "Lord Nelson is no more!" was repeated with such despondency and heartfelt sorrow that everyone seemed to mourn a parent. All exertion was suspended; the veteran sailor indulged in silent grief; and some eyes evinced that tenderness of heart so often concealed under the roughest exterior.'

Admiral Collingwood, when told of the death of Nelson, had at once taken over command. To do so he had been forced to move to the *Euryalus*, his flagship the *Royal Soveriegn* being left with no mast on which to hoist his signals. Immediately he ordered that the two most valuable prizes, both now disabled, should be taken in tow. The *Thunderer* took the *Santa Ana*, flagship of the Spanish Admiral de Alava, and the *Prince* the four-decked *Santisima Trinidad* with her 130 guns.

The British ships, now totally dismasted, included the *Tonnant* and the *Belleisle*, both of which had suffered so disastrously under the first broadsides of the enemy's attack. The *Spartiate* took the *Tonnant,* the *Naiad* the *Belleisle.*

Night coming on, the *Naiad* frigate took us in tow, wrote Nicolas, and the next day endeavouring to get into the Straits of Gibraltar, we lost sight of the fleet.

14

THE ENDLESS NIGHT

The *Belleisle* was the only British ship totally dismasted. Her hull was literally knocked to pieces; scarcely a spot in her sides, bows, or stern, appeared untouched;- all her ports, port-timbers, chain-plates, channels &c., were cut to pieces; and she was exceedingly leaky from shot holes.

In this state it seems miraculous that she could stay afloat even in the calmest of seas.

Nicolas describes the terrors of what next occurred: 'After the decks were cleared we were employed in erecting jurymasts to keep the ship under command, and before dark we had a few small sails set for the purpose. The sea and wind had increased with every appearance of a heavy gale coming on. The ship laboured excessively, and in spite of the constant exertions of the frigate we drifted fast towards the shore. Several times the tow-rope parted, but notwithstanding the risk of approaching an ungovernable hulk in such a tremendous sea, a line was thrown and repeatedly the hawser was again hauled on board the frigate.

'The increasing storm had driven us so near the shore that it appeared almost beyond human hope that we should escape the frightful prospect before us. About midnight a midshipman entered the wardroom, where most of our cots were swinging, to say that the Captain wished the officers to come on deck, as it was probable we should be ashore very shortly. This awful intelligence was received with much concern, and we instantly started on our feet. Just at this crisis one of the twenty-four pounders out of the stern-port broke adrift from its lashings, and the apprehension of our danger had taken such entire possession of our minds, that the crash appeared to announce the approach of our destruction. With difficulty I got on deck. The ship rolled in the trough of the sea in such a manner that the water came in through the ports and over the waist hammock-nettings, and the shot out of the racks were thrown about the decks, on which the men, tired and exhausted, were lying. At one o'clock the roar of the elements continued; and every roll of the sea seemed to the affrighted imagination as the commencement of the breakers.

'The hours lagged tediously on, and death appeared in each gust of the tempest. In the battle the chances were equal, and it was possible for many to escape; but shipwreck in such a hurricane was certain destruction to all, and the doubtful situation of the ship kept the mind in a perpetual state of terror.

'In this horrible suspense each stroke of the bell, as it proclaimed the hour, sounded as the knell of our approaching destiny, for none could expect to escape the impending danger. In silent anxiety we awaited the fate which daylight would decide; and the thoughts of home, kindred, friends, pressed round the heart and aggravated our despair. Each brightening of the clouds, which appeared as if to mock our misery, was hailed as the long-looked for dawn, and sank our wearied hopes into deeper despondency as the darkness again prevailed. How numerous were the inquiries made to the sentry, "how goes the time?" and when the welcome order to strike two bells (that is five o'clock) was heard, it aroused our sinking energies, and every eye was directed towards the shore. In a few minutes "land on the lee bow! Put the helm up!" resounded through the ship, and all was again bustle and confusion.'

Lieutenant Owen, describing how 'during the middle watch the breakers were seen on our lee bow' says 'At this time our fate appeared inevitable: two guns on the main-deck had broken loose, and were with difficulty choked up by the seamen's hammocks; the ship was altogether unmanageable, and gradually drifting towards the surf, the roar of which added to the horrors of the scene. At this juncture a few gallant men, under the superintendence of the second lieutenant, Thomas Coleman, with uncommon exertion and perseverance, erected a small spar on the forecastle [they erected the jib-boom on the stump of the foremast] on which they hoisted a boat's sail, by aid of which the ship was wore, and Captain Hargood congratulated me on being safe, as her head was in her new position a little off shore; still she drifted towards the breakers.'

124

'When we got round,' writes Nicolas, 'the breakers were distinctly seen about a mile to leeward, throwing the spray to such a terrific height that even in our security we could not behold them without shuddering.'

He then describes the reaction of himself and his fellow shipmates to their escape from almost certain death:

'This was a period of delight most assuredly: but intense dread had so long overpowered every other feeling, that our escape from destruction seemed like returning animation, producing a kind of torpor which rendered us insensible to our miraculous preservation; and it was not until the mind had recovered its wonted calmness, that our hearts were impressed with a due sense of the merciful protection we had experienced.

'As the day advanced the wind abated, and the enlivening rays of the sun well accorded with our happiness. The Naiad, having us in tow, spread all her canvas, steering a direct course for Gibraltar; all fears had then ceased, and the glad faces seemed to anticipate nothing but pleasure as they turned towards the object of our destination.

'This enjoyment, near as it appeared, however, was again interrupted by a cry of "a sail ahead," followed by "she looms large," and soon confirmed by "a ship-of-the-line!" The consciousness of our own weakness magnifies every object of terror, and often blinds us to the resources that may still be at our disposal. The stranger must it was supposed, be an advanced ship of the squadron which escaped to the southward; and so confidently did the Captain believe it that a consultation was held, when it was resolved to destroy the battered hulk and make our escape in the frigate. Preparations to carry this decision into effect were about to be commenced, when the private signal dispersed our hasty fears, and we then recollected that Admiral Louis had gone to Tetuan for water.

'The Rock opened to our view about eleven. On the preceding evening the Governor (had) received information by a market boat of the defeat of the combined fleet, and in honour of the victory he had directed a salute to be fired by the garrison. When we arrived near our anchorage, the battery of the Devil's Tongue commenced firing, and a *feu-de-joie* followed along the lines; each ship manned her yards and cheered as we passed; and our entrance into the mole was very gratifying: crowds of every class came to greet and congratulate us, and to learn particulars of the victory which had been

125

gained. The contrast between the appearance of our ship at that time, and the bright sides and majestic beauty which marked her proud course only a few days before, was very striking even to an indifferent observer: but to those who felt identified, as it were, with her fortunes, the reflection of her helpless condition and the honourable scars she bore, made a grateful and lasting impression:- we had endured danger and suffering but we had triumphed.'

Allen says:

'the Belleisle carried if not the first at least the most detailed intelligence of the glorious victory of Trafalgar to Gibraltar. At this place the badly wounded were landed, and such repairs of the shattered ship as could be effected here, were done.'

Nicolas is more explicit: 'Disabled ships continued to arrive for several days, bringing with them the only four prizes rescued from the fury of the late gale.'

Collingwood had been forced to order the scuttling of the huge *Santissima Trinidad*, the greatest warship ever built, flagship of the Spanish Rear-Admiral Don Baltazar Hidalgo Cisneros, before she went on the rocks.

'The anchorage became covered with ships,' continues Nicolas. 'In the mole lay six dismasted hulls, whose battered sides, dismounted guns, and shattered ports, presented unequivocal evidence of the brilliant part they had taken in the gloriously contested battle; a little beyond the more recently arrived lay at their anchors. At this proud moment no shout of exultation was heard, no joyous felicitations were exchanged, for the lowered flag which waved on the *Victory*'s mast, marked where the mourned hero lay, and cast a deepened shade over the triumphal scene. The exertion which was necessary to refit the ships did not, however, permit the mind to dwell on this melancholy subject.'

The *Belleisle* was jury rigged, having a maintopmast for a mainmast, foretopmast for a foremast, a jib-boom for a mizen mast, and a spare spar for a bowsprit; and thus refitted she sailed for England in company with the ship which contained all that was mortal of the great hero – Nelson. The Victory, under escort of the Bellerophon and the gallant old Belleisle, – fitting protectors for her noble freight,- wended her way to the

126

shores of Britain; and having sailed from Gibraltar, on the 4th November, arrived in the Channel on the 1st December, when the Belleisle and Bellerophon quitted her, and entered Plymouth Sound on the 2nd. Being found in want of complete repair, she was paid off on the 14th January, 1806.

Nicolas describes his own homecoming in the *Belleisle*: 'As we were the first who took the returns of our killed and wounded, nothing was known of our loss by our friends until our arrival, although several ships had preceded us; their suspense can be imagined, for the anxious enquirer only knew that our ship had suffered severely. Each day our protracted arrival increased their solicitude, hoping, yet dreading, as the eager eye watched the signal that announced approaching ships.

'At length we reached our destination, and arrived in Plymouth Sound on the 4th December. Boats innumerable floated round us with faces expressive of the torturing anxiety which was felt, and a moment ensued of such boundless joy to many, and bitter agony to others, that no pen can describe it: it would have wrung the most callous heart.

'I could not bear to hear the effusions of grief which burst from the childless parent, or witness the sorrow of brotherly tenderness, and I hastened to the affectionate embraces of my own family.'

What tales he had to tell them, this boy who was just sixteen.

15

'A CONCLUSION GRAND BEYOND DESCRIPTION'

Lieutenant Owen concludes his long and interesting letter with the following handsome but well merited eulogy on his captain: 'I will only add that he was so conspicuous for bravery, seamanship and presence of mind, during the whole course of these proceedings, as in justice to entitle his name to be handed down to posterity as one of the ablest and most gallant of the "Heroes of Trafalgar." '
A letter from Vice-Admiral Collingwood to Sir Peter was found among Hargood's papers:

> *Queen* off Cadiz.
> Nov. 1, 1805.
> My dear Sir Peter,
>   You will have seen from the public accounts that we have fought a great battle, and had it not been for the fall of our noble friend, who was indeed the glory of England and the admiration of all who ever saw him in Battle, your pleasure would have been perfect, that two of your own pupils, raised under your eye, and cherished by your kindness, should render such service to their country as I hope this battle will in its effect be. I am not going to give you a detail of our proceedings, which you have seen in the public papers, but to tell you I have made advantage of our calamities; and having lost two excellent men, I have endeavoured to replace them with those who will in due time, I hope, be as good. I have appointed Captain Parker to the *Melpomene* – which I am sure my dear Nelson would have done had he lived - his own merit deserves it; and it is highly gratifying to me to give you such a token of my affection for you.

It was a severe action; no dodging or manoeuvring; they formed their line with nicety, and waited our attack with great composure; they did not fire until we were close to them, and we began first. Our ships were fought with a degree of gallantry that would have warmed your heart – everybody exerted themselves, and a glorious day was made of it. People who cannot comprehend how complicated an affair a battle is at sea, and judge of an officer's conduct by the number of sufferers in his ship, often do him a wrong; [but] though there will appear great difference in the loss of men, all did admirably well, and the conclusion was grand beyond description, eighteen hulks of the enemy lying amongst the British fleet, with scarcely a stick standing, and the French *Achille* burning; but we were close to the rocks of Trafalgar, and when I made the signal for anchoring, many ships had their cables shot and not an anchor ready. Providence did for us what no human effort could have done – the wind shifted a few points and we drifted off the land. The next day bad weather began, and with great difficulty we got our captured ships off the land. The second day [Admiral don Federico] Gravina, who is wounded, made an effort to cut off some of the ships with the squadron of nine ships which he retired with. In the night the gale increased, and two of his ships – the *Rayo* 100, and *Indomptable* 80 – were dismasted; the *Rayo* anchored amongst our hulks and surrendered, the *Indomptable* was lost on the shore, and, I am told, every soul perished. Amongst such numbers it is difficult to ascertain what we have done, but I believe the truth is twenty-three sail of the line fell into our hands, of which three got into Cadiz in the gale of wind, viz. *Santa Ana*, *Neptuno*, and *Algeciras*. The *Neptuno* is on shore in Cadiz, and likely to be lost there. Three we bring off safe, viz. The *Ildefonso*, *St. Juan Nepomuceno*, and English *Swiftsure*; and seventeen burnt, sunk, and destroyed. Four flag officers and plenty of commodores were our prisoners: Villeneuve, the Commander-in-Chief, I send home; Vice-Admiral de Alava, being dangerously wounded, I left in his ship, *Santa Ana*, and she drove into Cadiz; Cisneros, Spanish Rear-Admiral, is now in Gibraltar, but I intend he should go to England; Magon, the French Rear-Admiral, killed.

The storm being violent [and] our own ships most of them

in perilous situations, I found it necessary to order the captures – all without masts, some without rudders, and many half full of water – to be destroyed, except three which were in better plight; for my object was their ruin, not what might be made of them. As this filled our ships with prisoners, and the wounded were in a miserable condition, I sent a flag in to the Marquis Gitano, to offer him his wounded men, which was received with every demonstration of joy and gratitude, and two French frigates and a brig were sent out for them. In return he offered me his hospitals, and the security of Spanish honour, that our wounded men should have every care and every comfort that Spain could afford; so that you see, my dear sir, though we fight them we are on good terms.

But what had most astonished them is our keeping the sea after such an action, with our jurymasts and crippled ships; which I did the longer to let them see that no effort of theirs can drive a British squadron from its station.

God bless you, my dear Sir Peter, may you ever be happy,

Your affectionate and faithful friend,

Cuthbert Collingwood.

The *Belleisle* had hardly reached shore at Plymouth before Prince William, Duke of Clarence, was putting quill to paper.

Bushy House, Friday night.

Dear Hargood,

I congratulate you from the bottom of my heart, that you have at last had an opportunity of convincing your brother officers of those merits which I have long known you to possess. Everybody that had the honour and glory of sharing in the action, speak and write in the highest terms of the *Belleisle* and her gallant commander: to me it is a matter of great satisfaction that my old shipmate is so well thought of.

I hope to see you that we may converse over the action, and that I may be master of the subject; besides I must consider you as a child of my own, and we are to celebrate the victory here, which I have not yet done till you can be present. I wish another brave fellow could have witnessed our rejoicings – but he is gone: I mean my friend Nelson. You knew well my attachment and friendship for him, and you can, therefore, easily conceive what I must have felt, at the moment of the most brilliant victory, to lose my friend covered with glory, and entitled to the first honours of a grateful country. I did not think it was possible, but for one of my dearest relations, to have felt what I have, and what I do still, for poor Nelson.

I shall now conclude as I trust to see you shortly; but I must request you will let me know the day that we may arrange your reception. You cannot refuse the pleasure to several young ladies and gentlemen who talk of nothing else but "the brave Captain Hargood".

Adieu, and ever believe me,
Dear Hargood
Yours sincerely
William.'

There is little doubt that the invitation here so kindly given was accepted . . . on all occasions Sir William Hargood was a welcome guest at the table of his royal friend, which welcome was still continued when, at a subsequent period, his former captain became his sovereign.

Allen does not refer to it but it seems almost certain that Hargood was among the hundred captains who attended Nelson's funeral in St Paul's Cathedral.

The *Victory* reached St Helen's in the Solent on 4 December. On board was Nelson's body, embalmed in brandy and spirits of wine by Doctor Beatty, the surgeon of the *Victory*, who had attended him as he died. Now people stood with bowed heads at the sight of the flag at half-mast.

Uppermost in the minds of most was the day, less than three months before, when they had seen him in his naval uniform, the decorations which had identified him to the marksman stitched to the coat, run down the steps to the barge which rowed him out to the *Victory*. Now the ship lay again at anchor with all that remained of the body of the hero, so mourned by the nation, on board.

Six days later, on the 10th, the *Victory* left St Helen's to sail for the mouth of the Thames. Heading up the estuary she was met by the yacht *Chatham*, sent by the Board of Admiralty to convey Nelson's body to Greenwich. Dressed in his full naval uniform, he was then placed in the coffin made from the mast of the *L'Orient*, the flagship of the French Admiral Bruey, who had died on board his ship in what was perhaps Nelson's greatest victory, the Battle of the Nile. The coffin from the *L'Orient*, encased in another of lead, was then finally sealed within a wooden shell.

The *Chatham*, with Nelson's flag from the *Victory* flying at half-mast, sailed up the Thames to London. There he was buried with full naval honours beneath the great dome of St Paul's Cathedral.

Admiral Pierre de Villeneuve, conspicuous in his French uniform, was among the many mourners who, on the day of Nelson's funeral, crammed the great cathedral to its doors.

The French prisoners, 210 officers and 4,589 men, were brought to England. Some were held in prison hulks on the Thames, others brought in to Plymouth went to Millbay Prison and the recently built Dartmoor Jail. Most of the officers were allowed parole. Villeneuve, told he could live in any town more than thirty miles north or west of London, chose Reading. There he remained for five months until, in April 1806, he was exchanged for four British post captains and allowed to return to France.

Once in Brittany he wrote to Admiral Decrès, the Marine Minister, asking him for instructions. He told him to go to Rennes and there await his word.

Arriving in Rennes, Villeneuve took a room at the Hotel de la Patrie to which address he believed the expected letter from Decrès would arrive. But days passed and nothing came.

Desperate as to his future, he is said to have written to his wife saying that his life was a disgrace, and death a duty, and begging her forgiveness for his suicide. However, nothing of this can be proved. All that is known is that he was found dead in bed in his hotel room. Blood covered his body. He had been stabbed six times and an ordinary table knife had been left, driven up to the hilt, in his heart.

Was it suicide? Did he hire an assassin to do the deed which he had not the strength or the courage to do himself? Or was it, as is widely believed, a case of murder on the orders of the Emperor who, intolerant of all incompetence, believed that Villeneuve, in failing to defeat Nelson, had not only betrayed him personally, but in doing so had dishonoured his country's cause?

THE FAR PURSUIT

War had not yet ceased. The battle of Trafalgar had, it is true, humbled the enemies of England, but they were not annihilated. France now hit upon the scheme of sending out squadrons of line-of-battle ships, to attack our homeward-bound convoys. Unable to meet our fleets she became the owner of privateers.

These ships of war were owned by men who held commissions to seize and plunder an enemy. If they could not sink merchant ships they did them as much damage as possible before carrying off the cargo which was then shared out, most democratically, among the crew. Risking the gallows if captured, many made fortunes which, in some cases, set them up for life, often as landowners in the West Indies and elsewhere.

The *Belleisle*, having undergone such repairs at Plymouth as her shattered state rendered necessary, was re-commissioned for Captain Hargood by Lieutenant Josiah Thompson, on the 13th February, 1806, and after great exertions the ship was got ready for sea on the 14th April, and sailed out of Hamoaze to Cawsand Bay.

On the 8th May Captain Hargood sailed with fresh provisions, vegetables &c, for the fleet off Brest, under Earl St Vincent; and on the 10th, having completed his task, he returned to Plymouth, where he was ordered to join Rear-Admiral Sir Richard Strachan's squadron, appointed to go in pursuit of Rear-Admiral Willaumez, who commanded one of the French squadrons alluded to.

Before he sailed a letter arrived from the Admiralty, dated May 9th, 1806, informing him that he was to be one of the recipients of the gold medal, awarded by the King, to the captains commanding the line-of-battle ships at Trafalgar.

Accordingly on the 19th May the *Belleisle* sailed with the squadron consisting of seven sail of the line, two frigates and a brig as detailed below.

Guns: 80

Câesar	Rear-Admiral Sir J.R. Strachan Bart.
	Captain Charles Richardson.

74

Belleisle	Capain William Hargood
Terrible	Captain Lord Henry Paulet.
Bellona	Captain John Erskine Douglas.
Audacious	Captain Thomas L.M. Gosselyn.
Montagu	Captain Robert Waller Otway.
Triumph	Captain Sir Thomas M. Hardy Bart.

36

Melampus	Captain Stephen Poyntz.
Décade	Captain John Stuart.

16

Fly	Captain William H. Dobbie.

On the 30th May the squadron arrived in sight of Funchal. From thence it stood over for the Cape de Verd Islands and on the 15th June anchored in Porto Praya Bay where it remained for four days.

Sir Richard Strachan's information of the motions of the French squadron was at this time very uncertain, for after leaving Porto Praya he cruised for some time between the Cape de Verds and Azores, and then proceeded to St Michael's where the squadron arrived on the 20th July.

At this latter place it is possible he learnt that M. Willaumez was then in the West Indies, for on the 22nd [July 1806], the squadron departed, and carried all possible sail steering for Barbadoes.

Joseph Allen, in an appendix, gives details of what had happened to the French ships which escaped from Brest on 14 December 1805.

Two squadrons had been formed from eleven sail of the line. One, commanded by Vice-Admiral Leissegues, had been scattered and destroyed off Santa Domingo by English ships commanded by Vice-Admiral Sir John Duckworth on 6 February 1806. The other, consisting of one 80-gun ship, the *Foudroyant*, five 74-gun battle-ships, two frigates and two brigs and commanded by Rear-Admiral Willaumez had cruised off Barbados, before, when heading back for St Helena, they too had been chased by Duckworth, but had managed to escape.

Willaumez had then headed for the Cape of Good Hope, totally unaware that it just been taken by Commodore Sir Home Popham and Major-General Sir David Baird. The British, hoisting Dutch colours on the fort, had lured one of the French ships, the 40-gun frigate *Volontaire*, into Table Bay where she was promptly captured. Willaumez, however, warned by a prize of what was happening, managed to put out to sea with the rest of his squadron. He had cruised for some time between Africa and South America searching for the India fleet. Nothing, however, had materialized and so, with his ships running desperately short of provisions (he had planned to refit at the Cape) he sailed for Martinique.*

Meanwhile Rear-Admiral, Sir Alexander Cochrane, Commander-in-Chief of the North American station, had got wind of what he was about, namely the capture of a large convoy of merchant ships assembling at Tortola, the island at the north end of the Caribbean chain.

Cochrane, who eventually inherited the Scottish earldom of Dundonald, was one of the most colourful characters of his day. Fiercely outspoken, he had already made tempestuous attacks on corruption within the navy during the war with France. At one point a Privateer himself, he was later to win fame in command of the Peruvian Navy.

At this time, having put to sea from Barbados on 6 July, he had caught sight of the enemy to the windward of the Virgin Islands. The English squadron then consisted of the 74-gun ships *Northumberland*, *Canada* and *Elephant*, the 64-gun *Agamemnon*, and the *Ethalion* and *Circe* frigates. The French ships, six sail of the line (most of them large two-decker ships) and two frigates, however, had the advantage of being to windward and, being faster sailers, had again escaped.

Cochrane, unable to catch them, had then headed with his

squadron for Tortola. He had escorted the assembled fleet of 250 merchant ships into a safe latitude, before returning to Barbados. Here, on arrival, he heard that two British squadrons, under the command of Sir John Warren and Sir Richard Strachan, were in pursuit of Rear-Admiral Willaumez in the West Indies.

Sir Richard Strachan, another impetuous commander, was the hero of the Battle of Cape Ortegal, fought off the north-west coast of Spain in November 1805. In this action he had captured four French battleships, the van of the Combined Fleet, which had escaped after the Battle of Trafalgar. For this he had been made a baronet and received a pension of £1000 a year. Renowned for his impetuosity there was nothing he liked better than chasing the enemy at sea

On 8 August Strachan's squadron arrived and anchored in Carlisle Bay, Bridgetown, Barbados. Then, on receiving more clearly defined intelligence of the cruising ground of the French, he left Barbados on the 12th in pursuit.

On the 18th, being then in latitude 20°48' N longitude. 63°40' W , Bermuda then bearing N. 4°W, distant 230 leagues, the squadron was overtaken by heavy squalls from the north-east, and the appearance of the weather threatened a hurricane. Sir Richard Strachan, however, heeded nothing beyond the object of his pursuit, which at this very time was not far distant from him; but he had with him officers whose experience taught them that dismasted ships would be of little service if the enemy was to be fallen in with.

The officer of the watch on board the *Belleisle*, which ship was then under a heavy press of sail, having observed the *Triumph* shortening sail, notwithstanding the signals of the Admiral then flying to make more sail, immediately reported the circumstance to Captain Hargood. By this time the *Triumph* had sent her topgallant masts down on deck, and was evidently preparing for a heavy gale. Captain Hargood knowing Sir Thomas Hardy to be in possession of an excellent marine barometer, felt assured that some great change had taken place in it, and therefore ordered the *Belleisle*'s topsails to be close-reefed, and the topgallant masts to be struck.

Just before noon one of the seamen, named Thomas Hardy,

a remarkable coincidence, fell overboard. A boat was lowered, and the poor fellow was picked up, but he was too much exhausted, and soon afterwards died.

Towards the evening the wind continued to freshen, but still the Admiral refused to take advantage of the caution of his captains, and was consequently fast going ahead of the *Triumph* and *Belleisle*. Every preparation for a heavy gale was made aboard the *Belleisle*; the storm staysails were got up and bent, and by eight o'clock at night the gale had so much increased that it was found necessary to heave the ship to, under them and the foresail.

At this time the Admiral bore from the *Belleisle* north by east, about three miles distant, and soon afterwards was dismasted. A short time before midnight it was found necessary to haul down the mainstaysail, the ship being so much pressed, and at twelve the foresail was also taken off her, and in attempting to furl it the sail was blown from the yard, and the ship had then only her mizenstaysail set. The gale was now truly awful, and came on in tremendous gusts which frequently threw the ship on her beam ends. Vivid lightning added to the grandeur of the scene.

At one o'clock in the morning the Admiral's light – which must have been the poop light – was seen bearing north-north-east, but soon after it was lost sight of; it was again seen bearing north at two o'clock, but after this it was seen no more. The *Belleisle* laboured exceedingly in the terrific gusts of the furious hurricane which was then blowing. She shipped several seas, and at three o'clock the mizenstaysail blew out of the boltropes. The main and lowerdecks were completely flooded, and the water made a fair breech fore and aft, so that the officer's chests in the wardroom were floating about, and it was found necessary to cut holes, or rather to scuttle the decks, to get clear of it. The chain-pumps were then manned and the ship was at length freed of the water.

Thus passed this dreadful night, but owing to the precautions which had been taken previously to the gale coming on, no greater damage was sustained. At five the wind shifted suddenly to the west-south-west, but as the ship was well prepared this sudden change did no harm.

At daylight it was found that the lower rigging was in a very dangerous state in consequence of the heavy straining of the masts, most of the throat seizings being broken and the end ones consequently drawn.

[Briefly, the shrouds, or large ropes that support the masts, were on the point of giving way, in which case the masts must have gone over the side; that is, have been broken.]

It was therefore absolutely necessary to bear up in order to secure the masts. The larboard quarter boat having broken from its lashings, was at this time swinging about to the great danger of the mizenmast, and was therefore cut away. The fore and maintopsails, close-reefed, were then set and the ship flew before the wind. As the daylight increased a line-of-battle ship was seen on the larboard beam, with her mizentopmast gone, scudding under bare poles; and another on the starboard quarter with only a foretopmast staysail set.

The topgallantmasts were now got on deck; and as there was no chance of seeing the Admiral [the *Câesar* having been dismasted he had hoisted his flag in the *Triumph*] Captain Hargood directed his course towards the appointed rendezvous of the Chesapeake. The gale continued but was rather more moderate for several days.

Chesapeake, in Virginia, is at the mouth of the great sea-inlet, Chesapeake Bay now crossed by both bridge and tunnel.

It was found, when the weather moderated, that several casks had shifted from the heavy leaking of the ship on the night of the 18th [August]. In the course of a few days the *Belleisle* arrived off Cape Charles, the point on the north side of the entrance, now crossed by a bridge/tunnel, of Chesapeake Bay.

The hurricane which had thus overtaken and dispersed and dismasted part of the British squadron, also caused similar but worse disasters to the French Admiral of whom the squadron was in chase. In 22° north latitude the same hurricane reached the French ships and scattered them completely, so that when the gale subsided M. Willaumez, in the *Foudroyant*, found himself in a dismasted ship, without a rudder and entirely separated from his squadron.

On the 5th September Captain Hargood was joined by the *Bellona* and *Melampus*, and with these ships under his command he continued cruising halfway between Capes Henry and Charles, at the entrance of the Chesapeake.

[Now an incident occurred which could have provoked a war with America.]

At five o'clock on the morning of the 14th of September Captain Hargood observed a ship of the line under jurymasts, inshore, and endeavouring to enter the river; upon which he immediately bore up. With the wind at north-north-east, he made all sail in chase accompanied by the *Melampus*. At six the stranger also bore up and stood in for the land; the *Belleisle* was accordingly cleared for action and every preparation made for anchoring the ship with a spring on her cable. At half-past seven Captain Hargood ordered a signal to be made for a pilot, as the ship was in very shoal water, and it was considered dangerous to stand further in.

At a quarter past eight the stranger was observed to run ashore, but without hoisting her colours, and at a quarter-before-nine, the *Belleisle*, having approached as near as was prudent, dropped her anchor in five fathoms water; and as the enemy had struck, or rather had never hoisted, her colours, it was considered she had surrendered. Captain Hargood sent the boats inshore to take possession of her.

At a quarter before ten o'clock the boats returned bringing the Captain M.le Veyer of the French 74-gun ship *Impetueux*. An American pilot shortly afterwards came on board the Belleisle, and it was probably Captain Hargood's intention to endeavour to get the *Impetueux* off. Shortly after noon, however, two strange sail were observed in the offing which he made sail to examine.

The *Melampus* was accordingly entrusted with the destruction of the French ship, which Captain Poyntz effectually performed. After removing the prisoners, who were put on shore at Norfolk, the *Impetueux* was set on fire and totally consumed

William Hargood's own version of this event is given in his despatch to the Admiralty which he wrote on the following day.

> *Belleisle*, off the Capes of Virginia.
> September 15, 1806.

Sir.

I beg you will be pleased to acquaint my Lords Commissioners of the Admiralty, that Yesterday morning at daybreak, being in company with his Majesty's ships *Bellona* and *Melampus*, endeavouring to fall in with Rear-Admiral Strachan, a line of battle ship was discovered to leeward, under jurymasts, standing in for the Chesapeake, to which we immediately gave chase. On perceiving us she bore up and put in for the land. At a quarter-past eight observed she had taken the ground; being then within one mile I came to anchor in about five fathoms of water, and immediately sent boats and took possession of her. She proved to be *L'Impetueux*, of 74 guns and 670 men, commanded by Monsieur le Veyer Capitaine de Vaisseau, one of the squadron that had been cruising under Rear-Admiral Willaumez, having separated from him, and four sail of the line more, with a frigate, as per margin. [*Foudroyant*, 80 guns, *Patriote*, 74 guns, *Eole*, 74 guns, *Cassard*, 74 guns, *Impetueux*, 74 guns, and *Valereuse* frigate] in about 22° N. long. 63° W., during the heavy gale of wind on the 18th and 19th ultimo, wherein she lost all her masts, bowsprit, and rudder, and was otherwise much damaged.

About noon, perceiving two suspicious vessels in the offing, I got underway with the *Bellona*, directing Captain Poyntz, of the *Melampus*, to receive the crew and set fire to her, which he completed before eight o'clock in the evening.

I have the honour to be, &c,
W.Hargood.

W.Marsden, Esq

James's *Naval History* [Vol. 4. pp 302,303] states bluntly that 'The capture and destruction of the *Impetueux* was certainly a breach of neutrality, and the French consul at Norfolk so considered it, by refusing to acknowledge her late crew as prisoners of war. He adds, however, that 'the affair happily passed off in the United States with very little notice.

'With respect to the law of the case we do not choose to venture an opinion; but it is necessary to assert that no gun was fired by the *Belleisle* (although it cannot be denied that the *Melampus* fired a broadside at her) except as a signal for a pilot. The surrender of the

French ship appears to us to have been voluntary, and consequently no breach of neutrality took place; but, whether this be the case or not, the following letter received by Captain Hargood from the Admiralty on his arrival in England, will afford sufficient proof of the opinion entertained by his superiors in reference thereto:

Admiralty Office
14th Nov., 1806.

Sir

I have received and laid before my Lords Commissioners of the Admiralty your letter of the 15th September last, stating the measures which you had adopted for the destruction of the French ship *L'Impetueux* when she ran aground near the Chesapeake; and I am commanded by their Lordships to signify to you their approval of your conduct, and that of the officers and men employed on that occasion

I am, Sir,
Your very humble servant,
Wm. Marsden.

Captain Hargood
Belleisle, Portsmouth.

'On the 24th September, a squadron of line-of-battle ships, under Sir John Borlase Warren, arrived off Cape Charles. Captain Hargood joined it and after cruising off the Chesapeake a few days in the hope of falling in with others of the dispersed French squadron, returned to Enlgand, where he arrived and anchored at Spithead on the 1st November.

'The *Belleisle*, after being docked and refitted, sailed again under Hargood's command, on the 20th January 1807 to join the squadron of Sir Alexander Cochrane. On the 20th February she arrived in Carlisle Bay, Barbados, where the Rear-Admiral was at anchor in the *Northumberland*, with the *Canada* and *Ethalion*.

After cruising for a few months, sometimes in company with the squadron and at others by himself, in the course of which he captured two or three privateers and recaptured a great many English merchant ships. Captain Hargood was ordered to change into the *Northumberland*.

141

This ship had been badly damaged on the 6th February 1806, when Rear-Admiral Duckworth had pursued and captured the whole of the French squadron of nine ships, commanded by Vice-Admiral Leissegues, off Santo Domingo. Now as Cochrane shifted his flag to the *Belleisle*, William Hargood, bade farewell to the ship on which he had served in such traumatic circumstances for just over three years.

Ordered back to England, he received instructions to take under his protection a convoy of one hundred sail of homeward-bound merchant ships, with which he accordingly sailed from Tortola on the 1st August 1807.

In her voyage to England the *Northumberland* had on board a great many French prisoners of war. Some ships of the convoy were much in want of men [therefore] Sir Alexander Cochrane, as was frequently the custom, permitted a few of the prisoners to volunteer for service on board the merchant ships. The masters of the ships, so receiving the men, signed an obligation to deliver them up to the first prison depot on their arrival in England.

Among the prisoners on board the Northumberland was a captain of a French privateer – a Creole – who had caused very great annoyance to the trade of the West Indies. Thus man, in the course of the voyage, suddenly disappeared and it was concluded he had fallen overboard and was drowned.

But just as the *Northumberland* with her convoy was about to enter the Channel, a complaint was made by one of the masters of the ships to Captain Hargood that there was a plan formed by the French prisoners on board his ship for overpowering the crew and carrying the ship into a French port.

Upon enquiry it was found that the principal person concerned in the design was the identical privateer captain who was supposed to have been drowned. It appeared that in a calm he had managed to drop overboard from one of the lower deck ports of the *Northumberland* (having secured his clothes in a well greased bag) and had swum to the merchant ship, the captain of which he deceived with some plausible tale, and who had suffered him to remain on board the ship.

'After having attempted in the above manner to repay the merchant captain's kindness, he was removed to the *North-*

umberland, and very properly placed in irons for the rest of the voyage to England.

The *Northumberland* arrived safely at Portsmouth, on the 30th September, with her valuable convoy, at which place the ship was ordered to be repaired. On her being taken into dock she was found to have been so severely handled in her engagement with the French squadron, that it would take some time to get her again ready, and the ship's officers, with the exception of the petty officers and marines, were drafted into the *Neptune*, Sir Thomas Williams.

17

THE CALL OF THE SEA.

Before sailing from England in Sir Richard Strachan's squadron, Captain Hargood had received the accompanying handsome letter from Lord Howick, enclosing the gold medal so well earned at Trafalgar:

Admiralty, May 9th, 1806.

Sir.

His Majesty having been graciously pleased to order medals to be given to the captains commanding line-of-battle ships in the action of 21st October, 1805, as a mark of his royal approbation of so distinguished a service, I have the honour of herewith transmitting one to you.

I beg to express the sincere pleasure I feel in being charged with his Majesty's commands on this occasion, and have the honour to be, with the highest regard,

Sir,
Your most obedient and humble servant,
Howick

Captain W. Hargood. R.N.

Captain Hargood had no sooner arrived in Portsmouth than he received a letter from the Admiralty, written at the request of Lord Mulgrave, then the first lord, asking if he would accept the situation of Pay Captain at that port. Subsequently two Commissionerships of Dockyards were also offered to him. Both offers were refused. His almost proverbial antipathy to anything relating to pounds, shillings and pence was quickly aroused . . . besides something remained to be done on his own element, whereon he had already spent thirty-four years of active life.

Accordingly the *Northumberland* being again ready for sea, and her complement having been made up by volunteers, and drafts from various ships, he once more, and for the last time, sailed from England in company with the *Resolution*, Captain Sir George Burlton, to join the fleet off Cadiz.

The *Resolution* parted company off the rock of Lisbon and joined Sir Charles Cotton.

The *Northumberland* had hardly joined the fleet, then under the command of Admiral Purvis, when her Captain received a letter from Lord Mulgrave, First Lord of the Admiralty, acquainting him that the honourable appointment of a Colonelcy of the Marines had been conferred upon him:

Admiralty, April 18, 1808.
Sir,

I have great satisfaction in acquainting you that his Majesty has been graciously pleased to give you the commission of Colonel of the Marines. I am happy in the opportunity of assuring you that this mark of distinction is, in my estimation, but a tribute of justice to your professional character; and that in humbly submitting your pretensions to his Majesty's gracious consideration, I was not unmindful of the distinguished part which the *Belleisle* bore in the glorious battle of Trafalgar.

I have the honour to be with the greatest esteem,
Sir,
Your most obedient and humble servant,
Mulgrave.

Captain Hargood.
H.M. Ship Northumberland.

Hargood was both delighted and touched by being made an Honorary Colonel of the Marines. Just how much it meant to him is vouched for by Allen who writes, 'knowing well its inestimable value, [he] entertained the highest regard for this corps. The appointment therefore – which he continued to hold until promoted to his flag – was often referred to by him with marks of extreme gratitude and pride. His respect for the marines was especially proved when

145

nominated to the Grand Cross of the Bath, for being entitled to supporters for armorial bearings. He chose the 'Sailor and Marine.'

Meanwhile, in May 1808, pleased as he was by Mulgrave's letter, Hargood had to endure the tedium of yet another blockade. The fleet under Rear-Admiral Purvis continued to prevent a squadron of five French ships of the line from leaving the harbour of Cadiz.

The political situation in Spain and Portugal had now been dramatically changed. In the previous year 1807, Napoleon had contrived to make a treaty by which Portugal was jointly occupied by France and Spain. Then, when his army had crossed the Pyrenees, he had annexed all the Iberian Peninsula. He had forced the Spanish King Ferdinand to abdicate. He had occupied Madrid and had proclaimed his brother Joseph King of Spain.

The Spanish people had endured this tyranny until, on 2 May 1808, they had risen against their conquerors. The supreme junta had assembled at Seville where, on 4 June 1805, in the name of the wretched Ferdinand, its members declared war against France.

This declaration no sooner became known to Vice-Admiral Rosily, who with the Neptune of 80 guns, *Algesiras*, *Argonaute*, *Heros* and *Pluton*, all 74 guns, plus the frigate *Cornélie* and a corvette was at anchor in the harbour of Cadiz, than he offered to leave that port if the British would allow him. This of course being refused, he quickly removed his squadron out of the of range of the powerful town batteries into the Carraca channel.

In the meantime negotiations had been set on foot between the Governor of Cadiz, General Morla, and Rear-Admiral Purvis who offered to stand in with his fleet and assist in the proposed destruction of the French squadron. This however was declined by the Spanish authorities, who considered themselves sufficiently strong to effect the object without any assistance.

On the 9th June the British fleet became spectators of the efforts of the Spaniards to free themselves from the remains of that fleet which in the hour of need has basely deserted them. The ships of this squadron, it will be remembered, had all shared in the defeat of Trafalgar, and had been ever since confined by the blockade of Cadiz. It was now that the

Spaniards were, in a small degree, taking their revenge for their losses on that disastrous day.

At three o'clock in the afternoon a division of Spanish gunboats and mortar vessels, as well as some batteries erected for the occasion at Fort Louis and the island of Leon, commenced firing at the French ships. The French Admiral returned the fire with much determination and the mutual cannonade continued until night when it ceased on both sides.

On the following morning hostilities were resumed and continued at intervals till two o'clock in the afternoon, when a flag of truce was hoisted on board the *Heros* and Vice-Admiral Rosily addressed a letter to General Morla proposing to disembark his guns and ammunition, and haul down his colours, upon the condition that he was to retain his ships and men.

Such terms as might have been expected were refused On the 14th the Spaniards, having by this time been strengthened by a 30-gun battery, and by numerous gunboats, again prepared to open fire upon the French squadron. Vice-Admiral Rosily, then finding it useless to contend any longer with the force both from within and without, struck the French colours, and the ships were taken possession of by the Spaniards.

Shortly after this event General Morla (who afterwards proved a great traitor) and the Spanish Commissioners, embarked on board a British frigate, in order to proceed to England to treat for peace with the English government.

They were warmly received in England where, on 4 June 1808, a peace treaty was signed with Spain.

Immediately, on news of this, the policy of the British Navy was reversed. That fleet and those cruisers therefore, which for so long a period had lingered with hostile intentions on the shores of Spain, were converted into protectors. Every effort was now used by the new but faithful allies of that country, to dislodge the French invaders wherever they were located.

General Spencer arrived in the month of August with a division of five thousand men, with orders to proceed to the Bay of Ayamonte to intercept the passage of French troops across the Guadiana, as it was considered probable the French in Portugal would march upon Cadiz. Captain Hargood, in the *Northumberland*, was ordered to join and co-operate with General Spencer, and accordingly proceeded to the Bay. However, certain movements in Portugal indicative of a similar wish to be rid of the invaders fattening upon their soil induced the French to forgo their intention.[Therefore] the *Northumberland* returned to Cadiz to rejoin the fleet.

Lord Collingwood, with his flag flying in the *Ocean*, arrived just at this time from the Mediterranean, in order to assist the cause of the Spanish patriots; but finding them already so prosperous he quitted Cadiz taking with him the *Northumberland*, *Excellent* and *Terrible*. On the 26th August these ships got underway from their anchorage in the Bay of Cadiz, and arrived at Port Mahon, Minorca, on the 10th September. From there Lord Collingwood stood over to join his fleet cruising off Toulon, under Rear-Admiral Thornborough, which he fell in with on the 12th.

Captain Hargood continued to cruise off Cape Sicié with the fleet until the 19th November. He returned briefly to Mahon for water before rejoining Lord Collingwood on the 25th and continued with him until the 7th December. Then a tremendous gale of wind came on which so damaged the ships, especially the *Ocean*, that the fleet was dispersed and Lord Collingwood bore up for Malta.

Captain Hargood – who was entrusted to lead the weather division of the cruising fleet – constantly maintained his station. In fact, a stranger to the care which was taken on board the *Northumberland* to maintain this position would have imagined the motions of one ship to have been inseparable from those of the other.

Before the Admiral parted company he telegraphed to the *Northumberland* for nearly two hours, giving Captain Hargood directions to act as senior officer with orders for every ship at Port Mahon in case Sir Edward Thornborough was not there.

So numerous and complicated were the signals that subsequently, on Lord Collingwood's arrival at Minorca, his Lordship expressed himself highly pleased at the directness with which they had been understood and his orders conveyed.

Captain Hargood remained at Port Mahon with the fleet

until the 2nd March 1809. Then he put to sea and cruised as usual off Toulon until the 2nd May [after which] he was dispatched to the Adriatic, with the 74-gun ships *Excellent* and *Montagu*, to look after some French ships supposed to have escaped from Toulon.

18

ACTION STATIONS: THE ADRIATIC AND THE MEDITERRANEAN.

It was now over six months since 31 October 1808, when Russia had declared war on Britain. The Treaty of Tilsit, which had allied France to Russia, had naturally resulted in enmity between Great Britain and the vast provinces ruled over by Tsar Alexander I.

The Treaty of Tilsit included secret articles whereby what Napoleon termed the 'Continental System,' a means by which British commerce could be blockaded on land, was to be extended to Denmark and Portugal.

Canning, informed of this through his spies, immediately sent a force under the Evangelical Admiral Gambier and General Cathcart to terrorize the Danes. The plan was successful, Copenhagen was captured, the Danish fleet overpowered and Napoleon could only expostulate that the British had attacked an innocent neutral country.

Meanwhile his new ally, Alexander I, unwilling to precipitate an attack on his own country, lay low like a hibernating bear. However, with the onset of freezing winter weather the fleet, commanded by Admiral Gambier, with Cathcart's soldiers on board, was forced to quit the Baltic Sea. Alexander then seized his chance. On 31 October 1808 war was declared against England by Russia, and on 18 December a counter-declaration was issued by Great Britain against Russia.

Vice-Admiral Seniavin, the Commander-in-Chief of the Russian fleet, after his successes over the Turks, quitted the Mediterranean in August 1807. Behind him he left Rear-Admiral Grieg and a squadron of line-of-battle ships, for the purpose of taking full possession of the island of Corfu, ceded by France to Russia by the Treaty of Tilsit. This squadron remained in the Mediterranean, and upon the declaration of war with England, joined the French Admiral – M. Ganteaume – at Toulon.

Another reason for sending Captain Hargood to the Adriatic was to co-operate with the Austrians in their struggles with the French, in which Russia was taking part with the latter.

In 1809 Napoleon for the second time within four years, marched down the Danube to enter Vienna as a conqueror. Previously he had met with little resistance, but this time the three Austrian armies, each commanded by the Archdukes Charles, John and Joseph, brothers of the Emperor Francis, put up a stiff fight. On the Danube meadows of Aspern, just outside the capital, the Archduke Charles won one of the few victories on land that Napoleon ever lost.[1]

Despite this Napoleon then regrouped his forces to overwhelm the Austrians. The Emperor Francis fled to Hungary, and on 13 May 1809 Napoleon again took possession of the Schönbrunn Palace. Here, on 14 October 1809 a peace treaty was signed. By its terms Austria lost not only its share of Poland, parts of Carinthia, Carniola and Croatia, but its Adriatic territories and some of its Germanic lands along the Bavarian borders. The Emperor Francis had lost almost three and a quarter million of his subjects by one stroke of the pen.

The initial success of the Austrian armies soon received a severe check when Napoleon arrived to take command of the French Army. The amazing charisma of the Emperor gave new spirit to his men. The Archduke Charles was compelled to fall back on Vienna, while the Archduke John was also repulsed and obliged to retreat into Hungary.

In the meantime Trieste, which was unprovided for defence, fell on the 20th May 1809, an easy prey to the light troops of General Macdonald's division, under the command of General Schilt.[2] The artillery taken by the French at Gorisia and Prevald was immediately forwarded to this seaport. It was forthwith fortified against any attacks by sea; and the whole line of coast shortly afterwards was in possession of the French.

Previously, on the 16th May, Captain Jahleel Brenton[3] in the *Spartan*, with the *Amphion*, Captain Hoste, arrived off Trieste. They found the heights of Optchina occupied by the French, and a Russian squadron of three sail-of-the-line – most probably a part of the squadron before alluded to – and a Turkish line-of-battle ship which had been captured, also two frigates and a corvette lying ready for sea.

The Austrian flotilla, consisting of two brigs and nine gunboats, were under sail in the bay, and a great many vessels of every description were in a state of the utmost confusion and distress.

Captain Brenton, thinking a junction would be attempted between the Russian squadron and a French squadron at Ancona, intended to have attempted setting the ships on fire with Congreve rockets. But calms prevented him from getting sufficiently near. [Therefore] deeming it necessary to return to the island of Lošinj which he had recently captured, he quitted Trieste for that place.[4]

Captain Hargood arrived off the island of Lusin on the 28th May 1809. He was joined by the *Spartan*, Captain Brenton, and the *Amphion*.

Captain Brenton immediately came aboard the *Northumberland* to give a full account of the state of Trieste (which the French had captured only a week before). He also gave it as his opinion that the Russian squadron lying there might be attacked with a prospect of success.

Captain Hargood lost not a moment in proceeding to that place with the squadron under his orders. The *Northumberland* was quickly prepared for action, and every preparation was made for anchoring the ships by the stern.

The ships of the squadron were as follows :-

Guns 74
Northumberland   Captain William Hargood
Excellent   Captain John West
Montagu   Captain Moubray, now
                 Sir R.Hussey

Guns 38
Spartan   Captain Jahleel Brenton
Amphion   Captain William Hoste

32

Thames	Captain The Hon.G.G. Waldegrave
Brigs	
Imogene	Captain William Stephens
Redwing	Captain E.A. Down

The squadron, led by the *Spartan*, carried all possible sail during the night, and by daylight on the morning of the 29th May had arrived within a few miles off Trieste; but very soon afterwards the wind had died completely away. This was most unfortunate for had the breeze lasted only another hour the attack might have been made with the greatest ease. Every exertion was used, by means of towing with the boats, to approach the enemy but without effect. A light breeze shortly afterwards sprang up, but owing to the extraordinary undercurrents to which the Adriatic is particularly liable, the *Northumberland* and other line-of battle ships were unable to make any progress.

Captain Hargood was furious, his frustration increasing as the ships of the Russian squadron were seen to be warping inside the mole. Even more exasperating was the fact that the enemy's troops at Trieste, obviously expecting an attack, were now throwing up batteries at the points where the ships would have to pass.

Captain Hargood's particular orders were not to injure the town of Trieste; and the knowledge of these instructions rendered his hopes still fainter. However, he caused every possible means to be restored to in order to make the attempt, nor did he relinquish the hope entirely until Captain Brenton, at about four o'clock in the afternoon, gave his decided opinion that an attack could not then succeed.

Captain Jahleel Brenton, later to become Vice-Admiral, was at that time, like William Hoste, famous as a frigate captain in the fleet. Joseph Allen, in his acknowledgements, also mentions Thomas Freeman Jessop, Hargood's secretary, who served with him on the *Northumberland*, presumably at this time. The first-hand accounts of these two men thus verify Allen's description of the actions in which Hargood was currently involved.

The reasons why Captain Brenton urged a withdrawal from Trieste are explained by Allen. He spoke in the knowledge that:

A short time previously (before the *Spartan* had left Trieste on the 16 May) in standing towards Trieste for the purpose of withdrawing the prizes we had sent in there, he had seen a detachment of the French army, said to consist of twelve thousand men, marching down from the heights of Optchina and taking possession of the town, by which we lost more than half our prizes. We had therefore every reason to suppose that a strong garrison of these troops still remained in Trieste, and that the works would be manned by them.

This force, formidable as it might appear, would not have prevented our complete success, could we have made a sudden and unforeseen attack. But, when for more than ten hours, the enemy had been making every preparation for a vigorous defence, the case was very widely altered.

The late Sir William Hoste and I were together the whole day, and I believe more than once in the course of it we went on the Northumberland together.

Hoste, one of Nelson's protégés, was renowned as the greatest frigate captain of his day. In 1807 he had been sent by Collingwood to the Adriatic where, with just four frigates, he had been able to dominate the entire sea, disrupting all the ship movements of the French and their allies. Collingwood had sent Hargood to his assistance. Captain Brenton writes:

'It became our decided opinion after two or three o'clock that all hopes of getting the Russians out of Trieste were at an end. When, at half-past four, my signal was made by the Commodore, and the question put to me "Whether the attack should be made?" I gave a decided negative, and declared that if I commanded the squadron I would not undertake it, and for these reasons:-

'That situated as the Russians then were, we must have been exposed to the fire of the broadside on going in, as well as to the fire of the batteries. [Also] that should we have succeeded in gaining possession of the ships, we should have found them in such a state as to render their removal improbable if not impossible. Our own ships must have been to a certain extent crippled; and had we landed our people in order to remove obstructions to getting off the Russians, or for the purpose of taking possession of the batteries, they must have been exposed to the musketry of concealed troops as well as to that of the Russian crews and whatever garrison the enemy might have had at Trieste; and our retreat might have proved very difficult.

'In this opinion Captain Hoste entirely agreed with me. I think he was not present when I gave it – indeed he could not have been, as I recollect Captain Hargood asking me if I had any objection to repeating what I had said before his first lieutenant; when I replied that "I would readily declare it before his whole ship's company." '

Previously to the foregoing communications having been made, at about half-past three, it was found necessary to anchor the *Northumberland* and the other line-of-battle ships, as the current, notwithstanding all their efforts, was driving them rapidly to the south-east.

At half-past four the ships were at length relieved from the current, and shortly afterwards the sea breeze as usual set in from the westward. However, as it was impossible for Captain Hargood, in the face of Captain Brenton's declared conviction of the futility of any attempt that could be made – a conviction it must be remembered, derived from a full and perfect knowledge of the localities of the harbour of Trieste, which were probably better known to Captain Brenton and his gallant associate Captain Hoste than to any other officers in the Mediterranean, he gave orders to weigh.

With disappointment visible in every countenance, the squadron therefore left the enemy in his security, but before quitting the bay, the Russian ships were observed to have struck their lower yards and topmasts, and to have hauled so close in towards the shore that they must have been aground.

From Trieste the Commodore bent his course for Pesaro off which place he arrived on the morning of the 31st of May.

Previously to the arrival of Captain Hargood to take command of the squadron in the Adriatic, Captain Brenton had attacked this place with great success and had demolished a fort at the entrance to the harbour, besides taking possession of a great many vessels deeply laden. However, he had not

155

succeeded in totally destroying the defences and the enemy gunboats and coasters were still using the harbour. [Thus] it was determined to renew the attack upon it with all the force that could be brought to bear.

Another reason for the attack was that the Austrian Archduke John was supposed to be not far from Pesaro, closely pursued by the French. [Therefore] it was hoped and considered possible that the cannonading of the town, which would be heard by the French, might have the effect of creating a diversion in favour of the Austrians.

The squadron arrived off Pesaro on the morning of the 31st and the Commodore made the signal for all the boats to proceed alongside the *Spartan*, to the captain of which ship the management of the expedition was committed.

The squadron, however, which it was intended should cover the boats in their attempts to enter Pesaro, was under the powerful influence of the extraordinary undercurrents experienced off Trieste. The *Northumberland* had studdingsails set, and a light breeze from the north-west filled all her sails, yet at twelve o'clock noon Pesaro was nine miles distant. The boats returned in the evening without having effected a landing, and the expedition was postponed until the next morning.

On the next day the squadron was more successful, and at a little before eight o'clock all the boats with the marines of the different ships, repaired alongside the *Amphion* and the smaller ships, which, being nearer to the town took the boats in tow and stood in for the shore, followed by the line-of-battle ships and the *Spartan*.

At about eleven o'clock the *Northumberland* and squadron anchored about a mile and a half off Pesaro, not being able to approach nearer on account of the shoalness of the water; the ships then opened their fire upon the town with visible effect, and continued without intermission till a quarter-past-one.

The boats returned at a little before two o'clock. On landing they had been received by a heavy fire of musketry, but the approach of the marines quickly put the enemy to flight, while the sailors set fire to several storehouses and stacks of timber.

The *Spartan* continued firing on the forts at intervals and the *Amphion*'s launch threw shells into the town; but from the shallowness of the water, which prevented the line-of-battle ships getting closer to the town, nothing more could be done there and the squadron quitted Pesaro for the island of Lusin, or Lusine, at which place it arrived on the 2nd June.

The *Spartan*, *Imogene* and *Redwing* parted company at this place for Malta, on the 5th. On the same day, the 7th June, Captain Hargood with the line-of-battle ships and *Amphion* also got underway and proceeded off Venice. On the 7th, Piran Point bearing east by south distant five or six leagues, the boats of the squadron were sent to chase a convoy of small vessels running down under the land. At half-past nine in the evening they returned triumphant, bringing two prizes and having burnt a gunboat and two other vessels.

On the 9th June the *Northumberland* and squadron stood close into Venice, where there were counted in the harbour two frigates, four armed brigs, and several gunboats. At eight o'clock at night the squadron came to an anchor off Piran Point where it remained till the next day. Having received intelligence that a large convoy was expected along the coast, it was determined to intercept it with the boats of the squadron and accordingly at midnight the whole stood in towards the shore.

Captain Hargood entrusted the command of the boats to the first lieutenant of the *Northumberland* – Mr James Leverick – an officer of experience and approved courage. The boats fell in with the convoy, and a very severe skirmish ensued, which unfortunately proved fatal to the gallant officer in command of it.

The case of this officer is very remarkable from the firm presentiment he entertained of his approaching end. A day or two previous to this attack, while walking the deck with one of his messmates, he remarked that if the ship got into action he felt sure he would not survive it. He was rallied for such an observation, and his brother officers, who well knew his courage, did all in their power to remove such an impression, but in vain.

When on the occasion the command of boats was given him, when quitting the wardroom his manner was remarked by all present. The purser of the ship in particular – who was sitting at the foot of the table and received from him a significant pressure of the hand at parting – was very much struck by his appearance. It was evident that his presentiment was not removed, but, notwithstanding its existence, it had no effect upon his public conduct. The barge in which he was pushed determinedly forward into the thickest of the fight, and boarded and carried one of the gunboats, in which, having left some of the barge's crew, he proceeded to the attack of the second. While in the act of boarding this he received a musket ball, which entered at his shoulder and taking a downward course lodged in the spine, from whence it could not be extracted.

The convoy, which was the strongest that had been known for some time, succeeded, after much hard fighting, in beating off the boats, and they returned in the morning to the ship bringing two other men who had been wounded, one mortally, in the action.

Lieutenant Leverick was placed in the Captain's cabin where he lingered for twenty-four hours in a state of extreme suffering which he bore as a brave man and a Christian. He died to the great regret of his captain and the officers and ship's company, by all of whom he was much respected. On his desk being opened a letter was found addressed to the purser, dated on the night he received his death wound, giving to his sisters the small property he had accumulated in the public service.

Despondent as they were, his shipmates had little time for mourning. On the night if the 12th June the boats were again dispatched and had a severe engagement with the enemy's gunboats. The pinnace was damaged by shot and a midshipman shot in the foot.

There was no letting up in the tension as the *Northumberland* lay in the Trieste roads sending the boats out every night to row guard. The anxiety of Captain Hargood, while on this harassing service, knew no respite; and the nature of his responsibilities was such as to call forth all his powers both mental and bodily. The coast being entirely in possession of an enemy, obliged him to be constantly on his guard. He was placed in an unenviable position, for the towns being those of a power believed to be friendly to England, although for the time under the yoke of a conqueror, were held sacred from molestation.

On the night of the 21st June the French brought down several field pieces to attack the boats, but the latter returned to the ships without injury.

On the 24th June, the *Northumberland* and squadron sailed for Fiume, when it was met by a heavy gale which caused great damage.

Captain Hargood continued thus actively and anxiously employed in the Adriatic until the month of August, in the course of which time the squadron was subjected to repeated attacks from the French troops occupying the coast. In the meanwhile the progress of Napoleon had been so great, and his victory at Wagram so overwhelming, that Austria, fearful of being brought into greater extremities, was induced to enter into an armistice, which was accordingly signed on the 18th July. The knowledge of this armistice was, however, withheld from the British until it was drawn out by Captain Hoste some weeks afterwards.

Allen, in a footnote, writes:

As Marshal Marmont approached Fiume, he sent one of his Aides-de-Camp to the municipal authorities to prepare immediately six day's rations for 10,000 men, and also a pair of shoes and a pair of trousers for each; or three million francs in money. This demand not being complied with, the town was placed under military requisition and parties of the military overran the town, and entered all the shops, from which they took all they could find. Such as was required by the Commissaries [the officers in charge of providing provisions and equipment] was applied by them, and such as was not required was sold to Jews and other followers of the camp. Before leaving the town the General sent for the Mayor or Prefect, and delivered him an account of all which had been taken from the shopkeepers, saying, "You now know the value: levy an impartial tax upon every inhabitant that these people be not greater losers than their neighbours."

On the 27th September, on quitting Fiume, prior to taking his departure from the Adriatic, Captain Hargood, having in company the *Excellent* and *Montagu*, was running down along the coast of Istria, In the afternoon, when not far from Pola, there was every sign of another storm coming on. The pilot on board the *Northumberland* undertook to take the squadron into the harbour which was considered to be the finest on the coast, and was intended by the Emperor Joseph to have been made into a great naval arsenal. But it was soon afterwards observed by the pilot's manner that he was ignorant of the proper channel, and the man soon confessed that he had mistaken the passage. The sail was instantly reduced, and as the ship was in six fathoms of water only, the anchor let go but too late to prevent her taking the ground. At 4.50 pm the *Northumberland* grounded on a sandbank between the small islands of Casadar and St Tereloma, the town of Fossano bearing about north. A strong current was at that time setting to the northward and every attempt to haul the ship off by means of her own and the *Montagu*'s stream anchors was found of no avail. At length the *Northumberland*'s bower anchor was carried out and added to the stream anchors but it was ten o'clock at night before she was hove off, without damage, the current by that time setting to the southward.

The *Northumberland*, being again in deep water, anchored, but in the course of the following morning a fresh gale came on during which the ship dragged her anchors and she tailed on the bank striking very heavily.

She was, however, still seaworthy and Hargood, on Lord Collingwood's orders, sailed for Malta on 19 October. He arrived on the 30th, just in time to be chief mourner at the funeral of his friend Sir Alexander Ball.

This was the man, one of Nelson's original ' Band of Brothers,' who, as the first British Governor of Malta, was so genuinely mourned by the Maltese that a handsome monument, in the form of a small Greek temple, was built to his memory on the ramparts over-looking the Grand Harbour of Valetta.[5]

19

SURPRISING THE SPANIARDS

While the *Northumberland* was lying in Malta harbour intelligence was brought that the French fleet had put to sea at Toulon. Instantly all was bustle, and the anxiety of Captain Hargood, who was senior officer, to put to sea was very great. The ship was in a few hours got ready for sea, and with the *Warrior* and *Magnificent* endeavoured to get out of the harbour, but a strong northerly wind effectually prevented this, although for several days their efforts were unrelaxed.

A change of wind at length enabled the ships to clear the port, and Captain Hargood sailed to join Lord Collingwood. He shortly afterwards learned that the French fleet had returned to Toulon, after losing two of their number destroyed by the squadron of Rear-Admiral Sir George Martin. Also a third line-of-battle ship and a frigate driven on shore had been much disabled. After cruising some short time off Cape Sicié, Captain Hargood proceeded to Port Mahon harbour, where he joined Lord Collingwood on the 1st December 1809.

Hargood found Lord Collingwood to be gravely ill. His condition grew steadily worse until, knowing that he lacked the strength to continue with the heavy burden of responsibility which the position of commander-in-chief entailed, he most unwillingly resigned.

Cuthbert Collingwood – Coll as Nelson called him - was one, if not the greatest, of the 'Band of Brothers' as his closest associates were described. A quiet reserved man, he preferred the company of his dog, a large animal aptly named Bounce, which sailed with him, to that of most human beings.

Nonetheless, despite his inherent shyness, he instilled such discipline into his crews that the 'cat' was seldom used. A perfectionist in everything connected with the navy, he was always reluctant to delegate, preferring to do everything himself.

This, in effect, killed him. Because of his huge work load he was exhausted, both physically and mentally, by years of constant responsibility, particularly arduous during times of war. Six years had passed since he had seen England. Now at last he had permission to retire. He longed for his home in Northumberland and to be with his wife and their two daughters who had grown up while he was away.

But his wishes were not to be granted. Sailing from Minorca to England, he died on board the *Ville de Paris* [a French ship captured by the English] on 7 March 1810.

Collingwood was succeeded by Rear-Admiral Sir Samuel Hood (cousin of his famous namesake, Lord Hood, with whom Nelson had first gone to sea). On 7 January 1810 Hood, with the fleet, including the *Northumberland* put to sea and returned to the old cruising ground off Cape Sebastian.

The *Northumberland* however, owing to her having been on shore, and her continual cruising, was by this time leaking badly. Sir Samuel Hood would have left her at Port Mahon, but that she could not be spared. The ship daily becoming worse, returned to Port Mahon to be surveyed, and the report of her surveyors was to the effect that she should return to England.

On the 1st March Captain Hargood rejoined Sir Samuel Hood, but the leak continued to increase until it amounted to thirteen inches an hour. On the 28th Captain Hargood parted company with directions to take under his orders the 120-gun ship *Hibernia*, which ship was also ordered to return to England on account of her being leaky.

Captain Hargood was entrusted with the execution of a very important commission on this passage, which was to endeavour to obtain possession of five Spanish line-of-battle ships in Cartagena. This was specifically to prevent their falling into possession of the French army, a division of which was then occupying Murcia, having defeated the Spanish General Blake and routed his army.

Captain Hargood finally sailed from Port Mahon on the 14th April, and on the 17th, in company with the *Hibernia*, arrived at Cartagena. Here the latter got aground as she was entering the outer harbour, and was with great exertion only got off after starting nearly all her water and taking out twenty of her lower deck guns.

Through the intervention of Colonel Doyle, with whom Captain Hargood was in close correspondence, on Saturday 21st April, leave was obtained from the Spanish junta by a majority of one only, to take away two of the Spanish three-deckers; but it was granted in such a manner that it was evident the greatest speed was requisite to prevent a revocation of the permission.

The state of the Spanish ships was such that it must have appeared an impossibility to get them ready for sea in less than several weeks. However, no sooner was the permission given than Captain Hargood dispatched three lieutenants, the master and boatswain and three hundred men in the service, with a like number from the *Hibernia*. They set to work late in the afternoon of the Saturday, and although the ships had their topmasts on deck and were wholly dismantled, they were completely rigged, with their sails bent, and warping out of the harbour on the Monday morning.

The astonishment of the Spaniards on witnessing such celerity, which must to them have appeared little short of miraculous, was very great. Indeed such progress would be scarcely credible to those who do not know the powers of British seamen when under the control of able officers. The two Spanish three-deckers – which were the *Ferdinand VII* and *San Carlos* – were conducted to safety to Gibralter, and moored inside the mole head.

The thanks of Sir Samuel Hood were conveyed to Captain Hargood in the subjoined letter:-

> H.M.S *Centaur*, off Cape Sicié,
> May 20th, 1810.

Sir,
I have to acknowledge the receipt of your duplicate letters of the 23rd and 24th April, informing me of your success in the execution of my orders, in prevailing on the Captain-General

of the Marine at Cartagena, to send away under your care the two three-decked ships, *Ferdinand VII* and *San Carlos*.

Your conduct on the whole of that service has given me the highest satisfaction, and I have no doubt it will be felt so by our superiors.

The Commander-in-Chief [Sir Charles Cotton, who arrived at Gibraltar in the *San Josef* shortly before the *Northumberland* sailed for England] who brought me your letter of the 5th instant, and the above mentioned duplicates, will have informed you of his full approbation of your services on the aforesaid occasion, which adds to the gratification I have experienced thereon; and it was not less pleasing to know from you the great exertions of the officers and men in fitting the ships out so speedily at such a critical juncture, and which only, it is probable, prevented the enemy's pursuing the grand object of an attack on Cartagena at that period.

I am, &c.

Samuel Hood.

Captain Hargood,
H.M.S. *Northumberland*.

Captain Hargood remained at Gibraltar until 1 June, when he sailed, still in company with the *Hibernia*, for England.

After a long passage, during which the *Northumberland* leaked as much as two feet of water an hour, he arrived at Spithead on 22 June and the ship was immediately docked. On 7 August Captain Hargood was included in the flag promotion and superseded in command of the *Northumberland*.

20

RESCUING THE PRINCESS:
THE SAILOR HOME FROM THE SEA

William Hargood was forty-eight when, in August 1810, he became a Rear-Admiral. A month later, thanks largely to the influence of the Duke of Clarence, he was appointed second-in-command at Portsmouth and hoisted his flag in the *Gladiator* in the harbour. The work involved was not of his liking – he was a blunt man who found dealing with rules and regulations irritating – but now that he was forty-eight he was becoming too old for the rigorous life of active service at sea. Perhaps the example of Lord Collingwood, worn out to the point of death, influenced his decision in accepting a posting on shore.

Transactions with the Admiralty made it necessary to go to London. He may have sailed there in the Admiral's barge, from Portsmouth round the coast and up the Thames. Alternatively he may have travelled on one of the stage-coaches, which, with frequent change of horses, travelled at about twelve miles an hour. On reaching the city he went visiting when business was done.

Hargood had maintained a longstanding friendship with James Morris, son of the Captain who had died after the attack on Sullivan's Island when Hargood himself was a midshipman in 1776. James Nicoll Morris, when Captain of the *Colossus*, had become a hero at Trafalgar. Badly wounded above the knee, he still walked with a limp.

The battle had taken place on the third anniversary of his marriage to Margaretta Sarah Somers Cocks, which had taken place in 1802. It is probable that it was he, who while on shore leave, introduced his friend William Hargood to his wife's younger sister Maria with whom he fell in love.

The sisters were the daughters of Mr Thomas Somers Cocks (brother of Charles, Lord Somers) a banker of Charing Cross. By 1811 the family were living at No 11 Downing Street, now the official residence of the Chancellor of the Exchequer. Here the little admiral, resplendent in his uniform, medals stitched to his coat, cocked hat under his arm, came to pay his respects. His feelings for Maria were reciprocated and despite the difference in their ages –he was nearly fifty and she at least ten years younger – they were married on 11 May 1811.

Portraits of the two sisters, done in watercolours enhanced with embroidery on a silk background, show them to be much alike. Both are wearing fancy dress. Maria - painted in 1789, when she was just grown up - seems to have been the prettiest. Her luxuriant brown curls, tumbling onto her shoulders, are crowned with a stylish top hat sporting a large cockade. Her feet are encased in tiny slippers and she carries a sprig of flowers.

Twenty-two years later, when she was married, she seems to have become a perfectionist as far as housekeeping was concerned. Hardly had the Hargoods settled in Portsmouth before Prince William, now the Duke of Clarence, with a large party of naval friends, came to dinner. Shortly afterwards, however, on 29 March 1813, her husband was made Commander-in Chief on Guernsey and hoisted his flag on board the *Vulture*.

Outwardly the island seemed very peaceful, a perfect place for a quiet life. Nonetheless Hargood's quick mind soon spotted discrepancies and after much interrogation he unearthed a network of intelligence and counter-intelligence which until then had been concealed.

It soon became apparent to him that the English government was much duped, and the revenue plundered by means of illicit traders, who under the plea of bringing intelligence relative to the French navy, were in fact seeking information to carry to that government and in the meanwhile were carrying on a thriving and safe trade.

The opinion formed by the Commander-in-Chief was conveyed to the Admiralty, and instructions were given him, which being carried judiciously into effect, in the course of a short time greatly reduced if they did not altogether annihilate it.

As this prohibition deprived many of the inhabitants of the islands of a fruitful source of emolument, it naturally made the Admiral for a time unpopular . . . but his sterling honesty soon satisfied all right-thinking people that public principle alone dictated his proceedings and in a short time restored to him that popular esteem which he so well deserved, and which it was generally his happiness to experience.

No incident of particular interest occurred during this command, which terminated at the peace in May 1814.

The armistice followed the defeat of Napoleon's army at the battle of Toulouse. The Emperor, having surrendered, was exiled on the island of Elba from where, as is well known, he subsequently escaped within the space of a year.

In the month of June Admiral Hargood [having returned to England] was nominated a Vice-Admiral of the Blue, and in January of the following year was created a Knight Commander of the Bath.

During forty-one years Sir William Hargood had been only three years out of employ; counting every day he had been on shore. His service may be said to have commenced with the first American war and to have ended with the termination of the second. In the interim France had declared war three times against England, in each of which Sir William had partaken, and distinguished himself. Now that war had ceased, although it was subsequently for a few months renewed, he retired for the first time into private life.

With his wife he went to live at Worthing but, because he was bored with a stationary existence they were constantly on the move. Brighton, and Leamington, were amongst the fashionable watering places which they visited. Eventually however, in 1817, they decided to live in Bath where they bought a house in Queen's Square.

Hargood was not the only retired sailor to find life on shore monotonous. He had only just settled in Bath when his old shipmate, the Duke of Clarence, arrived with his aged mother Queen Charlotte, whom he much resembled in looks, to stay in the town. Forced to dine with her, the Duke nonetheless used every possible excuse to escape from her company, going for long walks with his old friend Hargood nearly every day.

What memories the two sailors had to share. The festivities on the island of Nevis, when Nelson had married his pretty Fanny Nesbit, must have been some of the happier incidents about which they chatted as they stumped along.

Eventually, when the Queen announced she was leaving Bath, the Hargoods arranged a party for her son to take place on the following day. Many people were invited and lavish preparations made, but the sudden and unexpected death in childbirth of the Duke's niece, the Princess Charlotte, sent the whole nation into mourning and the party was cancelled forthwith.

The Hargoods were popular in Bath where they supported many charities and had what Allen describes as 'a select circle of friends.'

> Nothing of great event happened except that, in the severe winter of 1829–30, Sir William, walking to his club, slipped on the ice-covered street and broke his leg. He was carried home, and his own doctor being in the country, he refused to call in the assistance of any other, preferring to wait his return. The limb was in consequence rather inflamed, but it was at length set, and owing to the patience which he preserved throughout his confinement of many months, the bone reunited, and in the course of time the effects entirely wore off.

The Duke of Clarence, horrified by the news, at once despatched a letter in his own hand.

Bushy House,

January 30, 1830

My dear friend and valued shipmate,

Mrs Harper has just written to my unmarried daughter, mentioning that you have had the misfortune to break your leg; I must therefore write to enquire after you. This misfortune I have, thank God, not met with; but the dislocation of the shoulder, and the fracture of an arm, I am acquainted with, and are bad enough, but not by any means equal to your accident. I am anxious to know how you are, and request Lady

Hargood will answer this letter if it is at all inconvenient for you to write. I hope you will soon recover, and ever believe me.

Dear Hargood

Yours Truly,

William.'

Five months later, when George IV died on 26 June 1830, his younger brother William became King William IV. Almost immediately Sir William Hargood, being then in London, was summoned by the palace by the following note:

Sir Herbert Taylor presents his compliments to Sir William Hargood, and has been honoured with the King's commands to acquaint him that his Majesty will be glad to see him to-morrow at St. James's Palace at half-past four, and will desire Sir William Hope to bring him privately to his Majesty.

Bushy House, July 6, 1830.

Sir William thereafter dined frequently with his old friend who greatly preferred his company to that of the sycophantic courtiers who surrounded him. The King loaded him with honours.

On the 22nd March 1831 Sir William Hargood was decorated with the Grand Cross of the Hanoverian Guelphic, a personal honour conferred by his Majesty. On the 22nd July, he was raised to be Admiral of the Blue. And in September following, on the occasion of King William's coronation, the Grand Cross of the Bath was also added.

Notwithstanding his comparative seclusion Sir William still entertained the hope being again called into active service. Years might have weakened his bodily faculties, but his zeal was the same. At length his strong claims were recognised by Sir James Graham, the first lord of the Admiralty, from whom he received the assurance of the honourable appointment to the command of one of the principal seaports, in the subjoined communication :-

Admiralty,18th January, 1833.

Dear Sir,

I have received the King's gracious permission to offer to you the command at Portsmouth, vacant by the death of Sir

Thomas Foley. Your gallant conduct at Trafalgar – your long and faithful services – and the fact that you have not hoisted your flag since the peace, entitle you, in my humble judgement, to this distinction; and I am glad to communicate to you his Majesty's decision in your favour.

I.R.G.Graham.

It was first intended that Sir William should have the Portsmouth command, but Sir Thomas Williams, who about the same time was nominated to Plymouth, being anxious to have that at Portsmouth, and as Plymouth was preferred by Sir William, the exchange was easily affected.

[Therefore] On the 1st May, 1833, Sir William's flag was hoisted on board the 110-gun ship *San Josef** in Plymouth harbour.

Amongst the many friends who wrote to congratulate him on his appointment were Admiral Sir William Hotham, and his old shipmate Vice-Admiral Lord James O'Brien.

In 1812 the Scottish inventor Henry Bell had launched his steam-powered *Comet* on the Clyde. Seldom has any industry developed more quickly than that of steam-powered ships. Now, only twenty-one years since their introduction, steam vessels had become more widely used than sailing ships both for passenger traffic and trade. Likewise the navy was turning to their use.

Sir William, however, mistrusted them. Engines were not infallible. They could break down. They were not as reliable as sails. His views were forcibly expressed soon after his arrival at Plymouth – an incident already described in Chapter 10.

A lieutenant, who commanded a small brig, being ordered to proceed to the Sound, because the wind was rather scant, unadvisedly requested the Admiral to cause his brig to be towed out of Hamoaze by a steamship. Sir William with much energy

* The *San Josef*, formerly the *San José*, was a Spanish ship captured by Nelson at the Battle of Cape St Vincent. At the height of the action the *San José* was rammed astern by the *San Nicolas*, whereupon Nelson leapt from one ship to the other, one of his most famous exploits. Later, as the *San Josef*, she was his third ship in 1801. She remained in service until 1849.

in his manner, told the lieutenant that 'when in command of the *Belleisle*, had he not worked out of Hamoaze with the wind two points more against him, he should not have been at Trafalgar. He concluded by recommending the lieutenant to find his way to the Sound without delay.'

Hargood's mistrust of steam ships was soon to be justified.

Plymouth shortly afterwards became the scene of much gaiety in consequence of the arrival of the then Princess Victoria and her royal mother [the Duchess of Kent]. But the entrée of the royal party was attended by an accident which placed in extreme jeopardy the lives of the illustrious visitors. The following account of the occurrence alluded to is narrated by Captain Gordon Thomas Falcon, Sir William Hargood's flag captain, who, as well as Sir William, was present in attendance at the time. His version of the affair, differing in many points from generally received opinions, merits our best attention:

On the arrival of the cutter yacht, *Emerald*, on the 2nd August 1833, at Plymouth, . . . a most untoward accident, which was nearly proving fatal to the best wishes of the nation at large, took place.

The cutter in tow of a steam vessel, had arrived between St. Nicholas's island and the citadel when Admiral Sir William Hargood in his barge, attended by myself and accompanied by General Sir John Cameron and several others, repaired on board to pay the requisite homage and compliments to the royal party.

As it was previously arranged to land at the dockyard, and the breeze being very light, the yacht continued in tow of the *Messenger* steam vessel and proceeded towards Hamoaze; the flagship and every other ship in the harbour, manning yards and firing royal salutes as the yacht and her august passengers neared them.

It is proper here to mention that before getting among the shipping the hawser, by which the yacht was towed, ought to have been shortened in so as to give the steam vessel more power over the cutter, and enable her the better to counteract the various sets of the tide. The neglect of this precaution was

171

the real cause of the accident which followed. The consequence of this lack of foresight was that, arriving at the angle of the dockyard off which the first or outermost hulk was moored, the steam vessel having rounded the point and being so far ahead of the yacht, was immediately met by an adverse eddy, while the cutter being farther out continued under the influence of a strong flood tide. The steam vessel had also incautiously eased her paddles on rounding the point, which rendered her still more ineffective.

The yacht in consequence losing her way, and her rudder being rendered useless, drifted bodily towards the hulk. In another minute she dropped athwart the bows of it, but being driven ahead by the force of the tide, all her larboard chain-plates were torn off by coming in contact with the hulk's stem. The cutter's farther progress was stopped by her mast, which caught the cat-head of the hulk.

The strain upon the cutter's mast was very heavy, while the only support it could receive was from the forestay. Had it fallen it is more than probable that many lives would have been lost, for it happened that the boom remained topped up, and the mainsail hoisted, with the tack triced up, so that all was depending upon the strength of the forestay and mast, as all would have fallen with the mast.

Pandemonium reigned, but Hargood, as ever, kept his head, telling his Flag Captain to order his own barge to come alongside. This was done as quickly as possible but the crisis was not over. Falcon continues to explain what happened next:

In the meanwhile, perceiving the damage done to the rigging, and entertaining doubts that the strength of the stay was sufficient to withstand the unusual strain upon it, and being then close to Princess Victoria, I requested to be permitted to place her before the mast, as being a less dangerous situation. To this her Royal Highness instantly assented, and when so placed I considered her to be in comparative safety.

The barge being at length ready, I escorted the Princess to the gangway. Here her Royal Highness met the Duchess, from whom, in the temporary confusion, the Princess had been for a minute separated (for the events here narrated all occurred in

172

the space of a few minutes) during which interval she had most anxiously enquired for her Royal Highness, saying Oh where is my mother! and tears of alarm and anxiety filled her eyes.

The Princess's relief was great again on seeing the Duchess, who in the meantime had been attended by some of the gentlemen near her. I had the honour of handing the Princess into the barge; and attended by the Admiral, the royal party landed at the dockyard in safety, where every preparation had been made for their reception.

The forestay held on most unexpectedly, although the iron strop on the stemhead was nearly severed in two.

The above are the simple particulars of the occurrence, of which, from the situation I was then in, and knowing well Sir William's zeal and quickness, I was not unobservant. But I neither wish to claim any more credit than is my due, or to deprive others of any part they may be entitled to.

G.T.Falcon.

Plymouth was *en fête* for the royal visitors, with the annual regatta taking place. On the 5th August Sir William entertained the Princess and her mother to breakfast at Admiralty House. Many notable people, including the Duke of Norfolk, were present and afterwards all were treated to a cruise round the Eddystone, in the Forte frigate. It was a beautiful day, a band played on the forecastle, and the sailors in their best white ducks, their pigtails flying, danced hornpipes and reels.

On returning to shore the naval, military and civil officers at Plymouth were presented at the Royal Hotel. Then the Hargoods and all the principal officers and their ladies were entertained to dinner by the Princess at the end of this memorable day.

The summer of this year was also remarkable for the contest between Don Miguel and Don Pedro* and frequent arrivals tended to keep alive the interest felt by all parties in the result.

Sir William became noted for his hospitality while holding the Plymouth command. For Prince Joinville, who came in

* Both claimants to the throne of Portugal

1835, he gave a splendid dinner which was returned by a grand fête on board the French frigate.

Again, when Nemick Pacha visited Devonport he and his whole suite were entertained in similar style. Prince Albert's cousin, the King Consort of Portugal on his way to Lisbon, put in to Plymouth where he again was shown every mark of respect that his rank and the shortness of his stay permitted.

The popularity the Admiral enjoyed while at Plymouth was very great, though wholly unsought; and the termination of his command was the subject of almost universal regret. Since hoisting his flag he had made many friends. One was the Earl of Morley who, on his retirement, sent him the following letter:

Saltram, 30th April, 1836,

My dear Sir William

I cannot tell you how very much I regret that a slight return of indisposition prevents my accompanying Lady Morley, this morning, to the Royal Hotel, whither she proposes going for the purpose of paying her respects to Lady Hargood and yourself.

I can assure you that we shall not fail to inform ourselves of the election which you may eventually make upon the subject of our last conversation, and that, whether it is in favour of Malvern, Cheltenham, or any other place, it will be a matter of particular satisfaction to us to seize every possible opportunity of directing our steps in such quarter, and renewing to you and Lady Hargood the assurances of our real esteem and regard.

I fear that what I am going to say may not appear very refined or delicate, but I feel myself impelled, by a sense of truth, to state to you, that I have lived here all my life, and of course remember not a few Port Admirals, and I never recollect a single instance of a command being terminated, which occasioned ... such a universal feeling of respect and regret.

Always my dear Sir William
Yours sincerely
Morley.
Admiral Sir William Hargood, G.C.B,. G.C.H., &c.

174

More publicly, the *Devonport Herald* declared:

> We believe it to be in our power to state without fear or contradiction that there never was a more liberal Commander-in Chief at this port; whether as regards the hospitality – the splendid hospitality – displayed as Commander-in Chief at the Admiralty House, or towards every public institution, or public or private charity in the neighbourhood. Sir William has taken nothing with him of pecuniary gain from his appointment, all has been bountifully and beneficially spread in these towns; but Sir William takes with him something which princes would fain enjoy, and that is a good name, based on the esteem of all, and the love and affection of the many. Zeal for the public service was no less marked in his everyday character. As a witness we have only to refer to the past week, when the port looked more warlike than for a long period before. In the words of the sailor we say "He has never slept on his watch."

The *Plymouth Journal*, likewise, having lauded the Admiral, added a tribute to Maria:

> No lady ever entered more warmly into the interests of the public charities of Devonport, nor more readily afforded relief to present distress than did Lady Hargood. Her departure will long be lamented in this town and neighbourhood.

Thus they returned to Bath, with good wishes ringing in their ears. The house in Queen Square had been sold, so another was bought in the Crescent which proved to be the Admiral's last home.

From Bath the Admiral wrote as follows to General Sir Herbert Taylor.

Bath, August 19, 1836.

My dear Sir

Sunday being the birthday of our gracious Sovereign, I am very anxious to make known my most dutiful respects to him, but not being aware how far it may be correct to address his Majesty, I have taken the liberty of writing to you, being well assured, my good sir, you will take an opportunity of mentioning my wish.

When I relate to you the reason of my being so interested in that day, I am certain you will forgive my troubling you. I had the honour of being one of the lieutenants of his Majesty's ship, *Pegasus*, then under his command at Newfoundland, when his Majesty arrived at the age of twenty–one, and did us [the officers] the honour of dining in the gun room now *fifty years ago*. I cannot therefor, but feel very anxious to make known to his Majesty my most sincere congratulations on his enjoying, after so many years have elapsed, good health, and on his reigning over a free and happy country; and that his Majesty may continue long to reign is the sincere wish of a grateful and old officer, who is sensible of many favours conferred on him by his Majesty.

I am now to thank you for your kind attention tome on all occasions, and remain,

My dear Sir Herbert,

Yours most sincerely
W.Hargood.

Sir Herbert Taylor replied at once:-

St. James's Palace,

Aug. 20, 1836.

My dear Sir,

I have not failed to submit to the King your letter of yesterday's date, which was very graciously received by his Majesty, who honours me with his commands to thank you for the kind expression of your good wishes and attachment, and to assure you of his continued regard for an excellent old ship-mate.

I have the honour to be with the greatest regard.

My dear Sir
Yours most sincerely

H.Taylor.

Admiral Sir William Hargood. G.C.B., &c.
Bath.

In 1837 Sir William received a very gratifying present from his friend, Rear-Admiral Ross, which was no other than a relic of the old *Belleisle*. It came with the accompanying letter.

Plymouth Dockyard, Devonport,
11th April, 1837

My dear Sir William

Will you permit me to present for your acceptance a small testimonial of my regard and esteem, and also as a memento of the grateful recollection I have of the many kindnesses I received at your hands during the time I had the honour of being under your command. And when I say that the services of the old *Belleisle*, which you so long honourably and gallantly commanded, cannot be too much valued, I trust some of the old timbers might not be unacceptable to grace your table of hospitality.

I therefore beg you acceptance of some bottle stands made from the timbers of a ship of such well-earned renown, from a faithful and sincere friend. &c. &c.

Charles B.H. Ross.

Sir William answered from London.:-

15 Hereford Street, Oxford Street.

My dear friend

Your letter of the 22nd I received yesterday, informing me of your having forwarded me a box, which arrived a few hours afterwards. I am at a loss, my dear sir, for words to express to you my sense of the very kind manner in which you have pleased to show that friendship which can never be forgotten on my part. The contents of the box – eight bottle stands made from the timbers of the old *Belleisle* – I must ever value; and your expressions relative to my conduct on that great day, when my oldest friend and commander-in-chief, the great Lord Nelson, with whom I had served as a midshipman, was killed, are also truly gratifying to my feelings.

I assure you I shall take care that your valuable present shall be carefully preserved, as well as your letter wherein you allude to my long services, which commenced when ten years old; and

I am fully sensible of your kindness in terming them gallant and honourable.

Your most sincere friend,
W.Hargood.

At length the days of Sir William Hargood drew to a close. Nothing but a constitution originally of the strongest, could have borne up under services so long and harassing. Sir William in his early life had undergone much hardship and endured much sickness. Indeed on one occasion, it is believed that when in command of the *Hyaena*, he was considered to be dead and was on the point of meeting a watery grave. [Nonetheless] in later times he was in enjoyment of a good share of health, which was probably in a great measure owing to his abstemious and temperate habits.

Early in 1839 Sir William's health gave symptoms of decline, but after spending June and July at Clifton, he returned to Bath apparently much renovated. At Bath he continued to follow his usual habits, taking his customary carriage airings till the cold weather, which at all times affected him, set in. However, he enjoyed the society of many of his particular friends until a few days before his death, and his cheerfulness and good humour never for a moment left him . . . to his wife, who was constantly by his side, he often expressed himself with grateful pleasure.

Sir William continued to come downstairs to breakfast and it was only on the 11th December – the very first day his afflicted wife was apprized of the dangerous nature of his complaint, water on the chest [pleurisy or pneumonia?] that he kept his bed . . . on the succeeding day, the 12th, calm and resigned, he sank into a placid slumber which was succeeded by the sleep of death.

Thus, at the age of seventy-seven years, William Hargood, who as a little boy aged ten, had gone to sea and had then lived a life of adventure which reads like fiction today, died peacefully in his own home.

Unlike Nelson, 'his oldest and greatest friend', the story of his passing did not make headline news. Yet William Hargood left his mark in history as the little captain of the *Belleisle*, upon whom, in the maelstrom of Trafalgar, Nelson so heavily relied.

Sir William left two nephews, upon one of whom, Captain

William Hargood, of the Royal Navy, devolved the task of returning, at the Queen's levée, the insignia of the Grand Cross of the Bath, which his uncle had worn with such pride. The Guelphic Order was returned to the King of Hanover.

Sir William lies buried in the Abbey Church in Bath. A headstone, commissioned by his widow Maria, gives a brief resume of his life. Then come these words:

> He was beloved by all around him.
> Kind and considerate to the distressed, his benevolence, active as unostentatious,
> Was at all times administered with Christian feeling.'

Thus runs the last tribute to a small but remarkable man.

Appendix

WHAT THE PAPERS SAID!

Newspaper reports differed amazingly according to which country they belonged. The *Gibraltar Chronicle* wrote:-

By H.M. ship the *Belleisle*, which arrived here from the fleet on the 24th instant, totally dismasted, we have learnt some further particulars of this glorious victory. Having first described in outline how the battle was fought, it then described the fates of the French and Spanish ships. "The *Argonauta*, a Spanish ship of 80 guns, struck to her [the *Belleisle*] of which she took possession, sending the master and sixty seamen on board of her. The second captain of the *Argonauta*, who is now prisoner on board the *Belleisle* says that the ship had 950 men when the action commenced, of which nearly 400 were killed or wounded before she struck her colours. The first captain [de Alava] was severely wounded and left in the ship.

Villeneuve he states to have been the commander-in-chief of both squadrons, and Admiral Gravina to have commanded the Spanish fleet. He heard that Admiral Gravina, whose flag was hoisted on board the *Prince of Asturias*, was severely wounded in the left arm, and that three of four hundred of the crew were killed or wounded. *The Victory* we are informed, had sixty men killed and wounded, and lost her mizenmast and foretopmast. The *Royal Sovereign* lost her main and mizenmasts, and some other ships are also dismasted; but in general our gallant fleet has suffered much less than might have been expected in an action so glorious and decisive, and where the loss of the enemy has been so tremendously great.

We have also the inexpressible satisfaction to learn that there is every reason to believe that the fears entertained for the safety of our disabled ships, and those of the enemy in our possession, are unfounded, as they were seen at anchor on the Spanish coast after the late gales of wind had abated; and there is cause to believe that we shall shortly be gratified in beholding those splendid trophies of our victory safely moored in Gibralter Bay.

The *Algeciras Gazette* contains the official account of the line of battle of the combined squadrons on the day of their sailing, from which it appears that there were eighteen French ships of the line and fifteen Spanish, in the

180

action of the 21st; of which eleven have found their way back to Cadiz, namely five French ships, names unknown, and the following six Spanish ships –*Principe de Asturias*, *Rayo*, *Justo*, *Leandro*, *Montanez*, and *Francisco de Asis.*

Though it is highly honourable to the bravery of the Spanish nation, we most sincerely regret to find that the loss, both in ships and men, on this occasion has chiefly fallen on them; they were unwillingly dragged into this contest by their *good and faithful* allies the French, who, as usual, were the first to fly and desert them in the middle of the action; it appearing from every account that four of the French ships were seen running away from the fight about two hours and a half after the battle began.'

Napoleon remains the prime example of a single-minded man of genius who could never, under any circumstances, admit to being in the wrong. Within his conquered countries publications of all descriptions were censored.

The first bulletin of the Grand Army, from the *Moniteur*, as it appeared in the Herald Headquarters, Cadiz, on 25 October 1805, is as remarkable for its audacity, and contortion of the truth as it is for the inventive imagination of its author.

HOW THE ENGLISH LOST TRAFALGAR
From the Naval Chronicle of 1805.

The operations of the Grand Naval Army second in the Atlantic those of the Grand Imperial Army in Germany. The English fleet is annihilated! Nelson is no more! Indignant at being inactive in port, whilst our brave brethren in arms were gaining laurels in Germany Admirals Villeneuve and Gravina resolved to put to sea and give the English battle. They were superior in number, 45 to our 33; but what is superiority of numbers to men determined to conquer? Admiral Nelson did everything to avoid the battle, he attempted to get into the Mediterranean, but we pursued and came up with him off Trafalgar.

The French and Spaniards vied with each other who should first get into action. Admirals Villeneuve and Gravina were both anxious to lay their ships alongside the *Victory*, the English Admiral's ship. Fortune always so constant to the Emperor, did not favour either of them. The *Santissima Trinidada* was the fortunate ship. In vain did the English Admiral try to avoid an action; the Spanish Admiral Oliva prevented his escape and lashed his vessel to the British Admiral. The English ship was one of 136 guns, the *Santissima Trinidada* was but a 74. Lord Nelson adopted a new system; afraid of combating us in the old way, in which he knows we have superiority of skill, as was proved by our victory over Sir Robert Calder, he attempted a new mode of fighting. For a short time they disconcerted us; but what can long disconcert his Imperial Majesty's arms? We fought yard-arm to yard-arm, gun to gun. Three hours did we fight in this manner; the English began to be dismayed – they found it impossible to resist us; but our brave sailors were tired of this means of gaining victory, they wished to board; the cry was "*A la bordage!*" Their impetuosity was irresistible. At that moment two ships, one French and one Spanish, boarded the *Temeraire*. The English fell back in astonishment and affright. We rushed to the flag-staff, struck the colours, and all were so anxious to be the bearers of the intelligence to their own ship that they jumped overboard; and the English ship, by this unfortunate impetuosity of brave sailors and their allies, were able by the assistance of two more ships that came to her assistance to make her escape in a sinking state.

Meanwhile Nelson still resisted us. It was now who should first board and have the honour of taking him, French and Spanish? Two Admirals on each side disputed this honour. They boarded his ship at the same moment. Villeneuve flew to the quarterdeck. With the usual generosity of the French, he carried a brace of pistols in his hands, for he knew the Admiral had lost his arm and could not use his sword. He offered one to Nelson. They fought, and at the second fire Nelson fell. He was immediately carried below. Oliva, Gravina and Villeneuve attended him with the accustomed humanity.

Meanwhile 15 of the British ships of the line had struck. 4 more were obliged to follow their example. Another blew up. Our victory was now complete and we prepared to take possession of our prizes, but the elements were this time unfavourable to us, a dreadful storm came on. Gravina made his escape to his own ship at the begining of it; the Commander-in-Chief, Villeneuve, and Spanish Admiral were unable and remained on board the *Victory*. The storm was long and dreadful. Our ships being so well manoeuvred rode out the gale. The English, being so much more damaged, were driven ashore, and many of them wrecked. At length, when the gale abated, 13 sail of the French and Spanish line got to Cadiz, the other 20 have, no doubt, gone to some other port, and will soon be heard of. We shall repair our damages as speedily as possible, go again in pursuit of the enemy, and afford them another proof of our determination to wrest them from them the empire of the seas, and to comply with his Imperial Majesty's demands of ships, colonies and commerce. Our loss was trifling, that of the English was immense. We have, however, to lament the absence of Admiral Villeneuve, whose ardour carried him beyond the strict bounds of prudence and by compelling him to board the English Admiral's ship, prevented him from returning to his own. After having acquired so decisive a victory, we wait with impatience the Emperor's order to sail to the enemy's shores, annihilate the rest of his Navy, and thus complete the work we have so brilliantly begun.*

* Permission to reprint this extraordinary article, hitherto unpublished except in its original form, has been kindly given by Rear-Admiral C.H. Layman. CB, DSO, LVO.

NOTES

Chapter 1

1   Penn, Geoffrey, '*Snotty*', Hollis & Carter, London, 1957.
2   Masefield, John, *Sea Life in Nelson's Time*, pp 80–1.
3   Ibid. p. 62.
4   Moresby, Admiral John., *Two Admirals. p. 70.*
5   Masefield, John, '*Sea Life in Nelson's Time. p. 81.*
6   Ibid p. 84.

Chapter 2

1   Joseph Allen calls this Long Island, apparently by mistake.
2   Lieutenant Anthony Pye Molloy was promoted to the *Thunderer* and the junior lieutenant, Sir Charles Edmund Nugent, eventually became an Admiral of the Fleet.

Chapter 3

1   Rogozinski, Jan., *Honour Among Thieves*, pp. 226-29.

Chapter 5

1   Lloyd, C., *The Nation and the Navy* p. 149.
2   White, C., *The Nelson Encyclopaedia.* pp.150–52.
3   *History of the Royal Navy*, ed. Peter Kemp, p.98.
4   Rodney in fact returned to England d to find himself superseded, thanks to the government having changed, political power being all-important in the Navy of those days. The dispatches describing the victory of the Battle of the Saintes arrived too late for the order to be rescinded and Rodney received his peerage as a form of compensation for the decision to demote him which should never have been made.

Chapter 6

1   White, Colin *The Nelson Encyclopaedia*, pp 219–20.

Chapter 7

1   The account of the massacre is transcribed from Allen's book *Memoir* of *Admiral Sir William Hargood*. Appendix B, pp. 260–67.

Chapter 8

1   Masefield, pp. 73–99.
2   Ibid, p. 132.
3   *Narrative of the Mutiny at the Nore*, written and published by Sir Charles Cunningham, pp.109–10.
4   McGrigor, Sir James, *The Scalpel and the Sword. The autobiography of the 'Father of Army Medicine'* ed. Mary McGrior. p. 76.

Chapter 9

1   A signal conveyed by flags asking for identification. This had been previously arranged so that only British ships and their allies knew the signal to reply.
2   This piece of sarcasm is in allusion to the gallant and well-conducted attempt of Captains Edward Cooke and Pulteney Malcolm, in the *Sybille* and *Fox,* at Manilla, in January, 1798.

Chapter 10

1   Masefield J., *Sea Life in Nelson's Time*, pp. 14–15.

Chapter 11

1   Lloyd, Christopher, *The Nation and the Navy*, pp. 184–5.
2   Evidently midshipmen.
3   Ibid, pp. 177–9.

Chapter 13

1   Pope, D., *England Expects*, p. 318.
2   Ibid, pp 314–318.

Chapter 14

1   Pope, D. *England Expects*, p.18.

Chapter 16

1   Bowen. F.C. The Sea Its History and Romance. P.124.

Chapter 18

1   Brook-Shepherd, Gordon, *The Austrians*, pp.36–7
2   An anecdote is related of the female cook of the British Consul. After her master had quitted, and as the French troops were entering, she took post at the gate of the town, and making choice of the first general or field officer whose countenance she liked, she recommended him to make the Consul's house, his quarters. Her object was to preserve it from destruction; and in this it appears she was successful, for not only was the house uninjured, but she preserved a valuable cow from being slaughtered, saying, "What will Your Excellency do for milk if the poor cow is killed?"
3   Captain Jahleel Brenton, later Vice-Admiral and subsequently Lieutenant-Governor of Greenwich Hospital, an institution devoted to the care of retired or disabled sailors.
4   On 22 May the Battle of Aspern was fought.
5   White, Colin. *The Nelson Encyclopaedia*, p.59.

BIBLIOGRAPHY

Allen, Joseph, *Memoir of the Life and Services of Admiral Sir William Hargood. G.C.B., G.C.H.* Printed for private circulation only by Henry. S. Richardson, Greenwich.

Bowen, Frank C, *The Sea –its History and Romance, Vol III* Halton & Truscott Smith Ltd.

Broome, Jack, *"Make a Signal"* Putnam.

Bush, Eric, *The Flowers of the Sea.* George Allen & Unwin Ltd, London, 1962.

Cambridge University Press, *The Cambridge Modern History, Vol. VI The Eighteenth Century.*

Kemp, Peter (editor), *History of the Royal Navy*, Arthur Barker Ltd, 1969.

Kent, Captain Barrie, *Signal! A History of Signalling in the Royal Navy*, Hyden House, 1993.

Lewis, Michael, *The Navy of Britain*, George Allen and Unwin Ltd, 1948.

Lloyd, Christopher, *The Nation and the Navy*, Cresset Press, 1954.

McGrigor, Sir James, *Autobiography*, Longmans, Green, 1861.

Masefield, John, *Sea Life in Nelson's Time*, 1905.

Penn, Geoffrey, *Snotty. The Story of the Midshipman*, Hollis & Carter, London.

Pope, Dudley, *England Expects*, Weidenfeld and Nicolson, 1959.

White, Colin, *The Nelson Encyclopaedia*, Chatham Publishing, 2002.

INDEX

188

191